easy world craft

Gifts to Make

easy world craft

Gifts to Make

A handy step-by-step guide

DK

LONDON, NEW YORK, MELBOURNE,
MUNICH, DELHI

Project Editor Katharine Goddard
Senior Art Editors Glenda Fisher, Elaine Hewson
Managing Editor Penny Smith
Senior Managing Art Editor Marianne Markham
Jacket Creative Nicola Powling
Pre-Production Producer Rebecca Fallowfield
Senior Producer Katherine Whyte
Creative Technical Support Sonia Charbonnier
Art Director Jane Bull
Publisher Mary Ling
Special Sales Creative Project Manager Alison Donovan

DK INDIA
Managing Editor Alicia Ingty
Editor Manasvi Vohra
Senior Art Editor Balwant Singh
Managing Art Editor Navidita Thapa
Pre-Production Manager Sunil Sharma
DTP Designer Satish Chandra Gaur, Rajdeep Singh

First published in Great Britain in 2014
by Dorling Kindersley Limited
80 Strand, London WC2R 0RL

Material in this publication was previously published in:
Craft (2012)

A Penguin Random House Company

A CIP catalogue record for this book is available
from the British Library

ISBN 978-1-4093-5437-6

Printed and bound in China by Hung Hing
Printing Co. Ltd.

Discover more at **www.dk.com/crafts**

Contents

Introduction

BEADING • SILVER WIREWORK • COLD ENAMELLING • AIR-DRY CLAY

• METAL CLAY • PAINTING GLASS • MOSAICS

It's surprising how easy it is to create fabulous gifts with just a few tools and components. From stringing beads to make a necklace, to decorating glass and ceramics, the following pages contain all you need to know to get you started.

The techniques included in this book definitely fall under the category of "designer DIY". Whichever you choose – jewellery-making, painting, stenciling, or mosaics – you can easily produce decorative and functional items to give to friends and family.

With just a little know-how and the desire to be creative, you can add texture, colour, and interest to plain glassware or a simple china item, transforming it, as if by magic, into a unique and desirable gift. Most high-street shops sell a basic range of white china at bargain prices, so once you've mastered the skills, you could even use your newly gained knowledge to produce an entire hand-painted dinner service! Alternatively, give a new lease of life to a set of tired-looking tea light holders (see pp.68–69); these can be transformed with just a little paint into colourful objects to suit all tastes.

If you're looking to make a special piece of jewellery, semi-precious stones, polymer clay beads and shaped silver wire are easily available and are not as costly as you may think. So now is your chance to experiment with techniques that are new to you. If you're a keen needleworker, the loom-woven cuff on pp.46–47 is sure to appeal as the beads are woven with a needle and thread on a bead loom using an age-old weaving technique.

By following the clear step-by-step instructions given here, you'll have made your own unique hand-decorated items in no time at all – great for giving away as presents or for enhancing your home. Be inspired to take the techniques further and create your very own designs. Handcrafted jewellery pieces, mosaics and glassware always make welcome gifts and can be given extra-personal touches by making each piece in the recipient's favourite colours and style.

Tools and Materials

Tools and materials

You may find that you already have some of the tools and materials needed to make jewellery, but you may need a number of specialist materials when working with glass, ceramics, and mosaics. For comfort and safety, work on a well-lit, clean, flat surface.

Beading

Flexible beading wire This strong nylon-coated wire is available in different thicknesses. Cut the wire with wire cutters and store it in coils as any kinks cannot be removed.

Wire Wire for making jewellery comes in different thicknesses and finishes such as silver- and gold-plated, sterling silver, and coated copper. 0.6mm (24 gauge) wire is suitable for many applications.

Bead reamer A diamond-tipped bead reamer will enlarge a hole in beads of various materials or file a jagged edge of a hole which could snag thread. For best results, moisten the reamer and bead with water before use.

Adhesive Dab superglue, clear nail varnish, or bonding cement on thread knots and the joins of jump rings and wire loops to secure. Use epoxy resin glue to stick jewels and findings to clay jewellery.

Embroidery scissors Use small, sharp scissors such as embroidery scissors just for snipping thread or fabric. Paper will blunt them quickly and never use them to snip wire.

Bead stringing thread This flexible, synthetic thread is very strong. It comes on a reel or card in a limited range of colours and thicknesses.

Beading needles These are very thin with a long eye. They are prone to bending and breaking easily, so have a selection to hand. Long and short beading needles are available.

Cord, thong, and narrow ribbons Thread beads with large holes onto suede, leather, or cotton thong and narrow ribbon. Shiny, round cord called rattail comes in 1 to 3mm (1/16 to 1/8in) thicknesses and lots of colours.

Ear wires These come in various styles such as fish hooks and ear studs, which have a loop below to suspend beads. Ear clips are available for unpierced ears.

Tag ends These three-sectioned metal pieces fold into thirds to secure the ends of ribbon, cord, and thong. The loop at the top can be fixed to a jump ring.

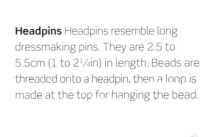

End bars Finish a multi-strand necklace by fixing each flexible beading wire with a crimp to a hole of the end bar. End bars can also be used to suspend beads from ear wires.

Fastenings Necklace and bracelet fastenings come in all sorts of styles and finishes, from simple bolt rings or a ring and bar to elaborate clasps festooned with jewels.

Jump rings Use these tiny findings to join fastenings to necklaces and to link components. Open and close jump rings sideways; do not pull the rings open outwards as they may weaken and snap.

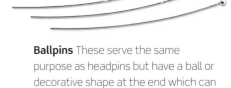

Headpins Headpins resemble long dressmaking pins. They are 2.5 to 5.5cm (1 to 2¼in) in length. Beads are threaded onto a headpin, then a loop is made at the top for hanging the bead.

Calottes Finish necklaces strung on thread with calottes, which consist of two hinged cups with a loop attached. The knotted thread ends are enclosed securely in the cups.

Bails Squeeze the claws of a bail through the holes of a drop bead. Some bails are very decorative and can coordinate with the style of the beads.

Ballpins These serve the same purpose as headpins but have a ball or decorative shape at the end which can be an added feature of your jewellery.

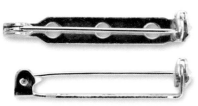

Brooch backs Stick a brooch back to the underside of a handmade clay design with strong epoxy resin glue. Allow the glue to dry completely before handling.

Crimps These tiny metal cylinders finish the ends of flexible beading wire on necklaces. Fix crimps with crimping pliers or snipe-nose pliers.

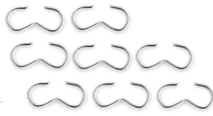

Figure-of-eight connectors Use these small components to join bezels that have a loop at each side to make a bracelet. They can also be used in place of jump rings.

Charms These small, decorative figures, usually made of metal, have a loop at the top ready for fixing to jewellery.

Chain This can be bought by the metre in various thicknesses and styles. Make a charm bracelet by fixing charms suspended on bails and jump rings to the chain, then fasten the ends with a clasp.

Jewellery stones and chatons To add sparkle, press jewellery stones and chatons into clay jewellery. Chatons have a gold foil backing. Flat-backed stones can also be glued to bezels and blanks.

Spacer beads Often made of metal, spacer beads can be placed between large beads. They are often an inexpensive way of adding more beads to a necklace.

Pearls Pearls have been popular for making jewellery for hundreds of years. Cheap realistic imitations are available in gentle colours and different shapes.

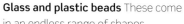

Tiny beads Use seed, rocaille, or Delica beads of the same size for weaving on a bead loom. Place a tiny bead between large beads of a necklace to help the necklace drape neatly.

Glass and plastic beads These come in an endless range of shapes, sizes, and colours. Plastic beads are lightweight, which is a consideration when making elaborate earrings.

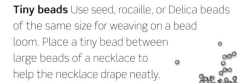

Crystals Swarovski crystals are the best quality crystals and so sparkly that just a few will set off a piece of jewellery beautifully. Facetted shapes such as bicones are particularly effective.

Drop beads and pendants These beads have a hole across the top and can be hung on bails to make pendant beads. Use handcrafted glass drop beads as a focal point on a necklace.

Jewellery maker's wire cutters Always use wire cutters to cut through wire and beading wire. Jewellery maker's wire cutters are easier to get close to small components than DIY-size cutters.

Jewellery maker's snipe-nose pliers Use these flat-faced pliers to close crimps, bails, and tag ends, and to help open and close jump rings. Crimps closed with snipe-nose pliers will be flat.

Jewellery maker's round-nose pliers Make loops in wire with round-nose pliers. Jump rings can be opened and closed by holding one side of the ring with a pair of round-nose pliers and the other side with snipe-nose pliers.

Jewellery maker's crimping pliers Although not essential, crimping pliers will close crimps on necklaces securely and neatly. They have two notches and make a neat, round crimp.

Cold enamelling

Cold enamel colours These can be mixed to create your own shades. The enamels harden in the air so there is no need for a kiln.

Cold enamel hardener Cold enamel colour must be mixed with hardener before use. For best results, always follow the manufacturer's instructions and leave to dry for 24 hours.

Jewellery blanks or bezels For a professional finish, apply cold enamel to ready-made metal bezels and blanks. A bezel has a rim to apply your decoration within; a blank is completely flat.

Loom weaving

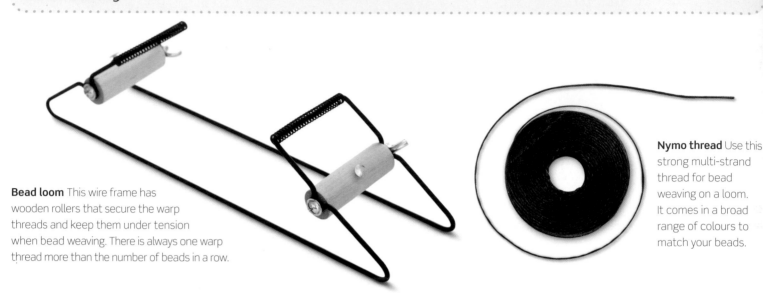

Bead loom This wire frame has wooden rollers that secure the warp threads and keep them under tension when bead weaving. There is always one warp thread more than the number of beads in a row.

Nymo thread Use this strong multi-strand thread for bead weaving on a loom. It comes in a broad range of colours to match your beads.

Polymer clay/air-dry clay/metal clay

Sanding tools Gently sand hardened clay to smooth any jagged edges with fine sandpaper and sanding pads. A needle file is useful for getting into intricate corners.

Rubber stamps and texture sheets There is a huge choice of ready-made rubber stamps and texture sheets available to press onto the surface of metal clay to create a design or texture.

Non-stick sheet A plastic stationery file divider is an ideal surface to work polymer clay, air-dry clay, and metal clay on. A Teflon sheet, or even playing cards, can also be used for metal clay.

Polymer clay This synthetic clay is hardened by baking in a domestic oven. There is a huge choice of colours, including glitter, translucent, and metallic versions.

Air-dry clay As the name suggests, the appeal of air-dry clay is that it hardens in the air. Some air-dry clays shrink a little as they dry out. Keep the clay wrapped in clingfilm and in an airtight container when not in use.

Tissue blade This long, thin blade is great for cutting all kinds of clay. A tissue blade is ideal for cutting straight lines or can be bent to cut a gentle curve. Keep the blade in a sealed container when not in use.

Cutters Small metal cutters allow you to stamp shapes from clay quickly and neatly. Cutters are available from craft and cookware shops.

Craft knife Cut clay with a craft knife when cutting around a template or an intricate shape. Change the blade regularly as a blunt blade will drag the clay.

Clay modelling tools An inexpensive set of clay modelling tools or synthetic clay shapers are very handy for shaping and smoothing clay. Even dressmaking pins can be used to create fine details.

Firing brick and mesh To protect your work surface, place metal clay pieces on a sheet of stainless steel mesh over a heatproof fibre brick while heating them with a torch. A small stainless steel cage, usually supplied with the steel sheet, can be placed over the clay.

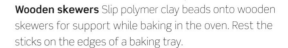

Tweezers Position small components such as jewellery stones on fresh clay with a pair of tweezers. Use the tips of the tweezers to embed the stones in the clay.

Wooden skewers Slip polymer clay beads onto wooden skewers for support while baking in the oven. Rest the sticks on the edges of a baking tray.

YOU WILL ALSO NEED...

Tape measure Use a flexible tape measure to judge necklace lengths and to measure lengths of beading. Popular necklace lengths are 40cm (16in), 45cm (18in), and 52 to 63cm (20½ to 25in).

Masking tape A piece of tape wrapped temporarily around the end of beading wire or thread will stop beads slipping off when threading.

Graph paper Work out a design on graph paper if you want a patterned length of bead weaving, with each square on the graph paper representing a bead.

Measuring cups Plastic drinking cups can be used to mix cold enamelling materials but for accuracy, use mixing cups with measure markings to measure quantities.

Mixing sticks and cocktail sticks Use purpose-made mixing sticks or cocktail sticks to mix cold enamel colours. Cocktail sticks are also used to pierce holes in clay and to apply superglue or clear nail varnish to secure jewellery findings.

Polishers and burnishers Polish metal clay with a stainless steel or brass brush, polishing pad, polishing paper, or polishing cloth to give it a shine. Burnish the metal with a metal crochet hook or the back of a teaspoon.

Clingfilm To stop clay from drying out, wrap spare clay in clingfilm while modelling the clay. For extra protection, store clay wrapped in clingfilm in an airtight container.

Non-stick roller Roll clay out flat with a non-stick roller. Small lightweight versions are available from craft shops. Keep the roller clean and only use it for craftwork.

Badger balm and olive oil Lightly smear badger balm or olive oil on your hands and tools when working with metal clay; they will stop the clay from sticking.

Talcum powder A light dusting of talcum powder on air-dry and polymer clay, or on your hands and roller, stops the clay from sticking.

Film and leadwork

A roll of self-adhesive lead These strips come on a roll and in different profiles (such as flat or oval). They have a peel-off backing. Even though they're metal they are quite soft and need careful handling. The narrower widths of lead come on a roll where they'll need cutting (along a guide line) to elicit the right width.

Sheets of coloured, self-adhesive film These sheets have a peel-off backing and are easy to cut using scissors or a craft knife. Smooth them down with a sponge or the side of your thumb nail.

Blu Tack This sticky stuff is great for positioning your paper design on the glass and holding in place.

Boning peg Available from the self-adhesive lead suppliers, this implement is perfect for the final pressing down and ensuring a good bond.

A fine permanent pen Trace your design onto the coloured film with a fine permanent black pen.

YOU WILL ALSO NEED...

Scissors Keep a pair of sharp paper scissors to hand; they're useful for cutting out the self-adhesive film and cutting lengths of lead strips.

Sponges Small scraps of sponge can be used for smoothing down sheets of self-adhesive film and easing out air bubbles caught underneath.

Sticky tape Useful for sticking film pieces to your duplicate design to keep track of your cutting out.

Scalpel and self-healing cutting mat For cutting self-adhesive lead or film for trickier or small shapes.

Painting glass

Methylated spirit Before embarking on a project, clean the glass inside and out with methylated spirit. This will degrease the surface so that masking tape and paint will adhere to it.

Glass to decorate Clear glass is the most versatile to paint on, but also consider coloured and frosted glass. Items to decorate could include tumblers, tea light holders, paperweights, bottles, and vases.

Scissors Keep a pair of sharp paper scissors to hand; they're useful for cutting out templates and snipping masking tape.

Tracing paper Use tracing paper to make templates to fit three-dimensional glassware. You can then create custom-made designs to trace onto the glass.

Masking tape Stick templates to glass with masking tape to hold them in place while you transfer the design to the surface of the glass.

Kitchen paper Rest the glass on a couple of sheets of kitchen paper for protection and to stop the glass rolling around. The paper is also useful to clean glass, wipe away mistakes, and mop up spills.

Glass paints These come in a range of vivid colours – water-based and oil-based versions are available. Some water-based glass paints can be fixed in a domestic oven; the results will be dishwasher-proof.

Craft knife Neaten any blobs of dried outliner with a craft knife. Don't neaten the line too much or it will lose its charming handcrafted appearance.

Old plate or white tile Mix paints on an old plate or white tile. You can mix water-based or oil-based paints together but do not mix the two.

Artist's paintbrushes Paint glass with good-quality medium and fine artist's paintbrushes. Clean the brushes immediately after use, washing off water-based paint with water. Follow the paint manufacturer's instructions to remove oil-based paint.

Glass outliner This is an acrylic paste piped from a tube. It creates a raised outline that contains the paint. Glass outliner is available in gold, silver, black, and pewter.

Painting china/tiles

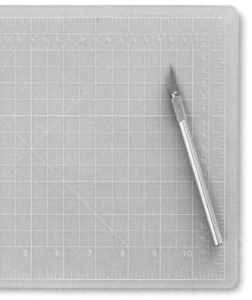

Card/thick paper Good for making stencils and sketching designs. For stencils, use thick paper or preferably card; anything too thin will get soggy.

Masking tape Useful for sticking stencils to ceramics and keeping them in place. Also use it to mask off areas you do not want to paint over.

Scalpel and self-healing cutting mat For cutting card or paper stencils with intricate detail, use a scalpel or craft knife over a cutting mat to protect the work surface.

Ceramic paints These specialist paints come in an array of colours. Pens are also available. Read the manufacturer's instructions to see how durable they are once baked.

Sponges Small scraps of sponge and even make-up wedges can be used for applying larger areas of colour and producing texture.

Paintbrushes A selection of shapes and sizes will give a variety of textures and brushstrokes. Experiment to see what effects can be achieved.

White bathroom tile This works like an artist's palette and is useful as a surface on which to pour small amounts of paint and for mixing colours.

Small jar or pot Dip paintbrushes in a jar of clean water to rinse them and prevent them drying out.

Rag/cloth Use an old rag to clean paintbrushes and wipe off any unwanted paint or colour.

Cocktail sticks These are useful for drawing or making scratch marks in wet paint.

Mosaics

Tiler's sponge These sponges are particularly dense. They are ideal for picking up surplus grout and make the job of cleaning the mosaic surface easier.

Small notched trowel This is used for applying cement-based adhesive to all backing materials when fixing paper-faced mosaic made using the indirect method. The small 3mm (1/8in) notches ensure that most of the surface is covered in adhesive, meaning that even small pieces will stick.

Plasterer's small tool This little trowel can be used to apply adhesive to flat and curved surfaces when using the direct method. The pointed end allows adhesive to be applied to awkward areas and can be used to scrape out excess adhesive.

Electrical screwdriver Useful for a multitude of tasks, from manoeuvring pieces into alignment to levering them off their backing.

Grouting float A good tool for spreading grout, particularly over large areas. It can also be used to press down on the mosaic to flatten out unevenness and ensure good contact with the adhesive.

Tile nippers This is an essential tool for mosaic cutting and can be used on all mosaic materials. The blades must be tungsten-tipped. It's worth paying a bit more to get a good pair that will cut accurately.

Double-wheel cutters These are primarily for cutting glass and give good, straight cuts. The blades can be turned when they get blunt so they last a long time. Replacement blades are also available.

Score and snap cutters These tools have a scoring wheel and a snapper for breaking the tiles. They are used when working with tiles larger than 2.5cm (1in) square to cut strips of the required size.

Found objects Popular found materials for mosaic include broken china and pebbles, but any small object can be used, including shells, marbles, beads, and buttons. Because found objects are usually irregular in shape, they are best used with the direct method and bedded directly into an adhesive bed.

Glazed ceramic Though small tiles only come in a limited colour range, you can get a much wider colour range in larger wall tiles then cut them down using a score and snap cutter. Glazed ceramic tiles are generally not frost-proof and only coloured on one side, so are best used with the direct method.

Washable PVA Polyvinyl acetate is a white liquid glue. The water-soluble variety, often sold as school glue, is used in a dilute form (50:50 with water) to stick tiles to paper in the indirect method.

Cement-based adhesive Tiling adhesives are based on traditional sand and cement but contain additives to improve adhesion and workability. Different types are available for different applications – always read the manufacturer's label to be sure you have the right product.

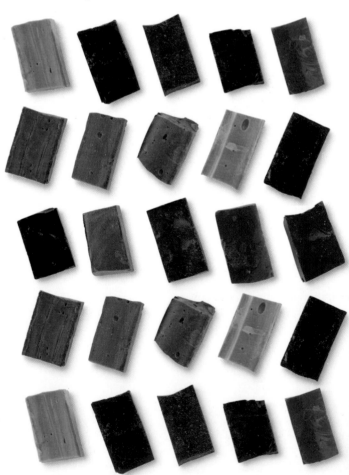

Smalti This beautiful enamelled glass has an uneven surface and a dense, often intense, colour. Usually available in 1.5 x 1cm ($^5/_8$ x $^3/_8$in) pieces, which can be cut with tile nippers and double-wheel cutters.

Cement-based grout Mosaics for practical locations, such as splashbacks, floors, and walls are grouted to fill the gaps between the tiles. Ordinary tiling grout is used, which comes in a range of colours, as well as white, grey, and black.

Unglazed ceramic mosaic tiles Unglazed ceramic is a hard-wearing material that can be used on walls and floors. Tiles come in two sizes, 2 x 2cm ($^3/_4$ x $^3/_4$in) and 24 x 24mm (1 x 1in), and in an attractive range of muted colours.

Vitreous glass
A popular and readily available material in a wide range of vibrant and subtle colours. The tiles are of uniform 4mm ($^3/_{16}$in) thickness and 2cm ($^3/_4$in) square, and can be used both indoors and outdoors.

Gold, silver, and mirror Metallic leaf sandwiched between a coloured layer of glass and a much thinner clear layer creates a durable, glittering surface. Cheaper alternatives are ordinary mirror or more recently developed versions that are protected with primer instead of glass.

Marble This soft stone can be cut with tile nippers, especially long-handled ones. It is often cut down from polished tiles into rods and then hand cut into cubes that can be used either on the polished face or on the honed (back) face. The sparkling riven (inner) face can also be used by splitting the cubes in half.

Brown paper Used in the indirect method as a facing for the mosaic tiles. Use strong paper: 90g is recommended.

Techniques
and Projects

Beading TECHNIQUES

A few basic techniques are all you need to assemble handcrafted jewellery. Keep pairs of jewellery wire cutters, snipe-nose pliers, and round-nose pliers to hand – they will help you achieve a neat finish to your jewellery. Although initially fiddly to handle, professional-looking wire loops can be made and jewellery findings attached quickly and efficiently with a little bit of practice.

Making a single loop

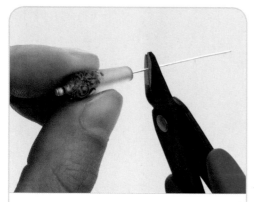

1 Slip a bead onto a headpin or ballpin, slipping a seed bead on first if the hole in your bead is too big. Snip off the excess wire 8mm (⁵/₁₆in) above the bead with wire cutters.

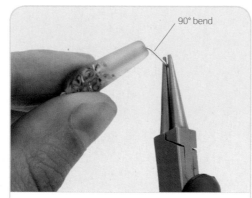

2 Hold the end of the wire with a pair of round-nose pliers. Bend the wire away from you at a right angle on top of the bead.

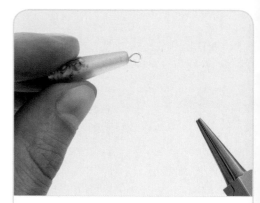

3 Turn your wrist to curl the wire towards you, making a loop. Release the wire, then grab it again to continue rolling it into a loop resembling a closed circle. A dab of superglue on the join will give added security.

Making a wrapped loop

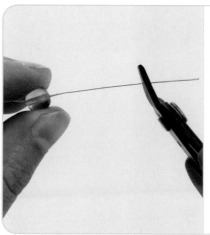

1 Slip a bead onto a headpin or ballpin. Snip off the excess wire with wire cutters, leaving 4cm (1½in) above the bead.

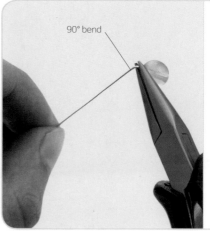

2 Hold the wire with a pair of snipe-nose pliers, resting the jaws on the bead. Use your fingers to bend the wire over the jaws at a right angle.

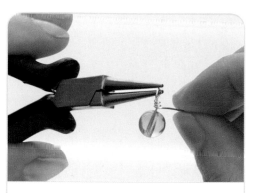

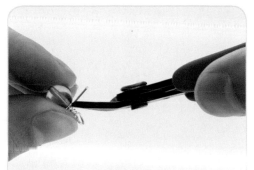

3 Using round-nose pliers, loop the wire around the jaw of the pliers so that the wire is at right angles to the wire emerging from the bead.

4 With the round-nose pliers through the loop to hold the piece steady, use your fingers to wrap the extending wire neatly around the wire emerging from the bead.

5 Snip off the excess wire close to the bead with wire cutters. Squeeze the snipped end close to the wrapped wire with snipe-nose pliers.

Attaching a bail

1 A bail has a claw on each side to hook onto a pendant or drop bead. Gently pull the claws of a bail open until the gap between them is large enough to slip a drop bead or pendant onto one claw. Slip the bead or pendant onto one claw.

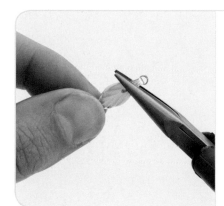

2 Squeeze the bail closed with snipe-nose pliers. Depending on the style of the bail, you may need to attach a jump ring to it (see below) to keep the component facing forwards.

Attaching a jump ring

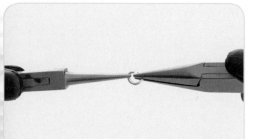

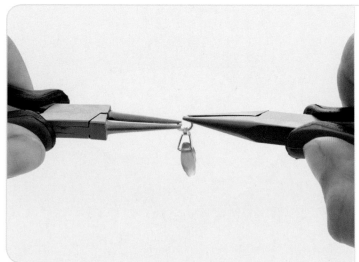

1 Jump rings join fastenings to necklaces and link components. Holding the jump ring between two pairs of pliers, gently pull one pair towards you until the ring opens wide enough to enable you to slip your jewellery component on.

2 To close, hold the open ring between two pairs of pliers and push one pair towards the other, aligning the join. For extra security, dab the join with superglue or clear nail varnish, using a cocktail stick to deliver a tiny amount.

Threading beads

masking tape

Wrap masking tape around one end of the beading wire or thread to stop beads slipping off. Thread on the beads, working outwards from the centre of your work. This allows you to add or remove beads either side of the centre to achieve the desired length.

Attaching a crimp

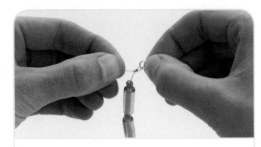

1 A crimp is a tiny metal cylinder used to fix the ends of flexible beading wire. Slip one crimp then one jump ring onto the wire. Pull the end of the wire back through the crimp until the crimp sits 4mm (³/₁₆in) from the last bead and the jump ring 4mm (³/₁₆in) from the crimp.

2 Place the crimp in the inner notch of a pair of crimping pliers. Squeeze the pliers closed; the squashed crimp will be crescent-shaped. If you do not have crimping pliers, squeeze the crimp flat with snipe-nose pliers.

3 Position the crimp in the outer notch of the crimping pliers. Squeeze the pliers closed to round the shape of the crimp. Turn the crimp and repeat to improve its shape.

4 Snip off the excess wire as close as possible to the crimp with wire cutters. If making a necklace, repeat at the other end.

Fixing calottes

1 A calotte has two hinged cups with a loop attached. The knotted ends of strung beads are enclosed in the cups for a neat finish. Insert the thread at each end of a necklace through the hole in a calotte. Tie the thread in a large knot and cut off the excess thread. Glue the knot in one cup of the calotte with superglue.

2 Squeeze the calotte cups closed with a pair of snipe-nose pliers. Slip the loop of the calotte onto a jump ring. Close the loop and repeat at the other end of the necklace, if this is what you're making.

Attaching a necklace fastening

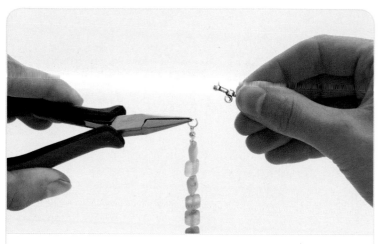

1 Use two pairs of pliers to open the jump ring at one end of the necklace. Slip the loop of one half of a necklace fastening onto the jump ring.

2 Close the jump ring using the two pairs of pliers. Apply a tiny dab of superglue or clear nail varnish to the jump ring join for extra security. Repeat at the other end of the necklace.

Attaching a tag end

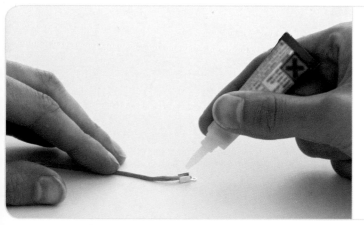

1 A tag end is a three-fold metal strip that secures the end of a thick threading material. Place the end of a cord, thong, or fine ribbon in the centre of a tag end. Glue in position with superglue. Allow the glue to dry.

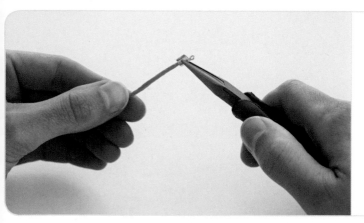

2 Fold one side of the tag end over with snipe-nose pliers, then the other side. Squeeze the tag end tightly closed with snipe-nose pliers. Fix a jump ring to the loop of the tag end.

Attaching an ear wire

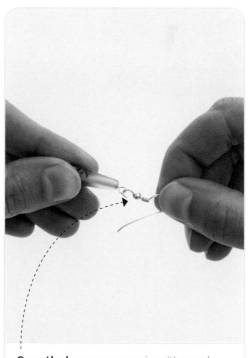

Open the loop on an ear wire with round-nose pliers. Hook the loop of the earring component onto the loop of the ear wire. Close the loop with the pliers.

27

Beaded pearl necklace PROJECT

A pair of delicate heart-shaped beads anchors two strands of pearls at the front of this beautiful necklace featuring classic pearls in gentle colours. Pearl beads often have very tiny holes, so use the slimmest beading needles for this project. Remember to thread on the same number of pearls either side of the hearts.

YOU WILL NEED

- 160cm (64in) white bead stringing thread
- embroidery scissors
- masking tape
- 2 short beading needles
- 2 x 1.2cm (½in) heart-shaped pearl beads
- 128 x 3mm (⅛in) natural round freshwater pearls
- 104 x 4mm (³⁄₁₆in) peach rice freshwater pearls
- 6 x 7mm (⁵⁄₁₆in) natural round pearls
- 2 gold calottes
- snipe-nose pliers
- 2 x 4mm (³⁄₁₆in) gold jump rings
- round-nose pliers
- gold toggle and ring necklace clasp

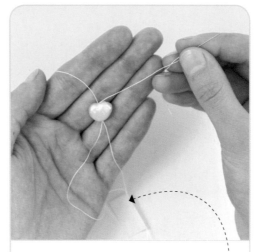

1 Cut two 80cm (32in) lengths of stringing thread. Join the threads with masking tape at their centre to stop the beads slipping off. As you'll be threading beads outwards from the centre, you'll be able to make changes to the beading sequence if you wish. Thread each thread onto a short beading needle. Thread both threads through the tip of a 1.2cm (½in) heart-shaped pearl bead.

2 Separate the threads and thread sixteen 3mm (⅛in) natural round pearls onto one thread and thirteen 4mm (³⁄₁₆in) peach rice pearls onto the other. Insert both threads through a 7mm (⁵⁄₁₆in) natural round pearl. Repeat this sequence twice. Separate the threads and thread sixteen 3mm (⅛in) natural round pearls onto one thread and thirteen 4mm (³⁄₁₆in) peach rice pearls onto the other.

3 Check the necklace length and how the pearls sit. If necessary, add or remove pearls. Tape the beaded thread ends and remove the masking tape at the centre of the necklace. Thread on the second heart and pearls to match the first half of the necklace.

4 Insert both threads at each end of the necklace through a calotte, then slip the loop of each calotte onto a jump ring. Slip the loop of the toggle clasp through the jump ring and close. Repeat on the other side with the second half of the clasp.

Beaded insects PROJECT

Hang butterflies and dragonflies from your blinds or curtains, or in your windows where they can sparkle in the light. They will also make lovely necklaces for little girls if hung from a thin ribbon, or can be used to decorate a lampshade for a child's bedroom. Make them as small or as large are you like, according to the size of beads you use.

YOU WILL NEED

- craft wire or 0.4mm (28 gauge) silver-plated wire, cut into 30cm (12in) lengths for each butterfly
- wire cutters
- 3–6mm (⅛–¼in) beads in assorted colours
- snipe-nose pliers (optional)
- 5–7mm (¼–⅜in)-wide ribbon in coordinating colours

1 Thread eight black beads onto the wire, then add one white bead – this will form the butterfly's body and head. Push the beads to the middle of the wire.

2 Thread one end of the wire back down through the top three beads and carefully guide it out of one side, as shown. Leave a small loop at the top to form a hanging loop.

bottom wire

3 Wrap the other end of the wire around the bottom bead and back through the others, pushing it out on the left-hand side. Thread beads onto the right-hand wire to make the top half of one wing.

4 Once you have threaded sufficient beads onto the wire for the top half of the wing, twist the wire around the body so that it stays in place. Repeat to make the lower part of the wing.

5 Do the same on the other side to create a matching wing. Bend all four segments of the wings so that they look as similar in shape as possible.

6 Twist the wires around the body to secure, and trim any excess wire with wire cutters. Thread a piece of ribbon through the top loop and tie in a knot.

Friendship bracelets PROJECT

Make your own colourful friendship bracelets – it's a great way to show somebody that they're important. As fun for beginners as it is for experienced crafters, these bracelets can be personalized to match the favourite colours of the recipient and adjusted to fit all wrist sizes. Add beads, ribbons and charms, and vary the designs according to whether you want trendy or vintage bracelets.

YOU WILL NEED

- suede twine or embroidery thread in a colour of your choice
- glass beads (optional)

Twine bracelet

1 Take two pieces of twine about the length of your arm. Make a loop in one and lay it flat, then wrap the second piece around it, as shown. Cross the two ends of the second strand over one another. Wrap them around the outside of the first strand and pull tight to make a knot.

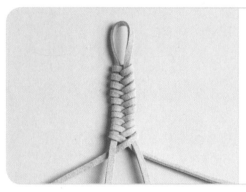

2 Repeat this process, crossing the ends over one another and going around the first strand until your bracelet is the desired length. Trim the ends. To add decoration, thread glass beads into your bracelet as you assemble it.

Embroidery thread bracelet

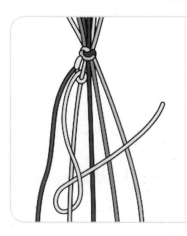

1 For a more complicated design, line up six lengths of different coloured embroidery thread, each about as long as your arm. Knot them together near the top. Take the first colour and loop it over and then under the second strand and pull it tight. Repeat this to create a double knot.

2 Do this again over the next colour, and then the next, until the first piece has moved all the way to the right side. Repeat this process with the second strand. Continue until the bracelet is long enough. Knot the strands together and trim the ends.

Silver wirework TECHNIQUES

Fixing beads on twisted wires or binding an item with wire threaded with beads is a great technique for decorating plain jewellery and accessories such as a hair comb, headband, or bangle, or to make pretty pendants to hang on a necklace or ear wires. Use 0.4mm (28 gauge) or 0.6mm (24 gauge) wire and always start and finish the wire on top of your work, so it won't scratch skin or clothing.

Making a bunch of twisted stem beads

1 Thread one bead onto wire, leaving a tail 5.5cm (2¼in) longer than the intended length of the longest twisted stem. Hold the bead and twist the wires together to 5cm (2in) from the tail end.

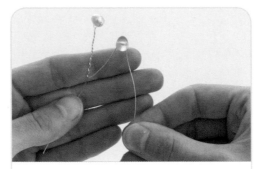

2 Bend the long end upwards and thread on another bead. With the bead just below the level of the first bead, twist the wires together under the bead until you reach the bottom of the first twisted stem.

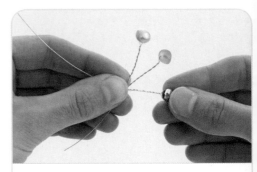

3 Again, bend the long end upwards. Thread on another bead and hold the bead just below the level of the second bead. Twist the wires together under the bead until you reach the bottom of the other twisted stems.

Binding with a bunch of twisted stem beads

1 Bend the short tail of wire of the bunch around the item to be bound, finishing on the outward-facing surface. Snip off excess wire. Squeeze the end flat with snipe-nose pliers.

2 Bind the long tail of wire of the bunch under and over the item a few times, pulling the wire taut as you work.

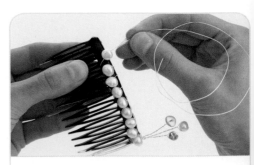

3 Continue binding the long tail around the item, adding beads if you wish. (See Steps 2 and 3 of **binding with wire and beads**, opposite.)

Binding with wire and beads

1 Leaving a 5cm (2in) tail, bind wire around the item four times to secure it. Snip off the tail on the outer surface with wire cutters. Squeeze the end flat with snipe-nose pliers.

2 Thread on a bead and hold it against the outer surface. Again, bind the wire around the item, pulling the wire taut as you work. Continue adding beads and binding.

3 If you run out of wire, bind the wire four times around the item, finishing on the outer surface. Snip off excess wire. Squeeze the wire end flat against the surface with snipe-nose pliers, then bind a new length of wire over the end of the last wire. Continue adding beads and binding.

Finishing a continuous binding

When you reach the end, bind the wire four times around the wire at the start. Finish with the end on the outer surface. Snip off the excess. Squeeze the end flat against the surface with snipe-nose pliers.

Finishing a straight edge binding

When you reach the end, bind the wire four times around the item, finishing with the end on the outer surface. Snip off the excess wire. Squeeze the end flat against the surface with snipe-nose pliers.

Making a pendant

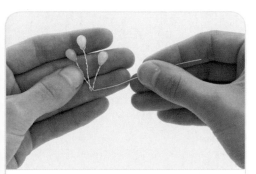

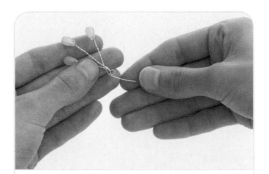

1 On a bunch of twisted stem beads, snip the short tail of wire level with the end of the twisted wires. Bend the other tail to a right angle.

2 Hold the tail with round-nose pliers close to the right angle. Roll the wire around the jaw of the pliers to make a loop. End with the tail at a right angle to the twisted wires.

3 Wrap the tail neatly around the twisted wires. Snip off the excess. Squeeze the end flat against the wrapped wire with snipe-nose pliers.

Pebble flowers PROJECT

A unique way to display photos and cards, these stylized wirework holders make eye-catching gifts. The pebbles can be left in their natural state or painted and varnished for a coloured design. You can make this project as dainty or chunky as you wish, using larger or smaller pebbles, but make sure that the wire is sufficiently strong to support your photos.

YOU WILL NEED

- flat pebbles, approximately 10cm (4in) in diameter
- silver- or gold-plated craft wire
- wire cutters or scissors
- snipe-nose pliers
- 2cm (³⁄₄in) buttons
- craft glue
- mini pegs
- photos or postcards (to display on your photo holder)

1 Wash the pebbles to remove any surface dust or grit. Paint the pebbles or varnish them, if you wish. Measure out approximately 100cm (40in) lengths of wire for each flower.

2 With the top of the button facing upwards, thread the wire through one of the holes and twist the end underneath to secure. Thread the wire back up through the second hole.

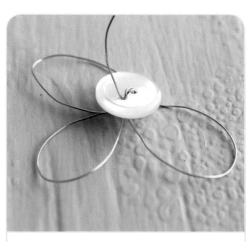

3 Thread the wire back and forth through the holes, bending it each time to make petal shapes.

4 Wrap the wire around the pebble, leaving a short length as a stalk, plus another short stub of spare wire. Twist to secure. Bend the wire stub upwards.

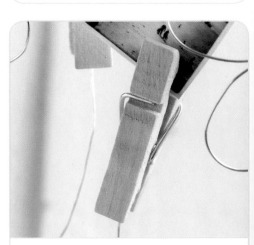

5 Glue one side of a mini peg to the wire stub. Once the glue is dry, clip a photo or postcard to the peg.

Sparkly tiara PROJECT

Make this pretty tiara to set off an outfit for a special occasion. Bunches of twisted stem beads stand proud of the headband and the sides of the band are bound with wire and beads. Bead shops sell plain tiaras ready to decorate, or use a narrow headband instead. A mixture of crystal, glass, semi-precious chips, and pearl beads have been used here, adding a touch of glamour.

YOU WILL NEED

- 8m (9yd) 0.4mm (28 gauge) silver-plated wire
- wire cutters
- selection of 3–6mm (1/8–1/4in) crystal, glass, semi-precious chips, and pearl beads in assorted colours
- silver-plated tiara or 5mm (1/4in) wide silver headband
- snipe-nose pliers

1 Snip a 1m (40in) length of wire. Follow **making a bunch of twisted stem beads** on p.34. Hold the bunch of twisted stems at the front edge of the centre of the tiara. Bind the short tail over and under the tiara. Finish on top of the tiara and snip off excess wire if necessary. Squeeze the end against the tiara with snipe-nose pliers.

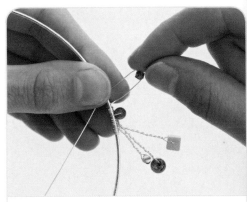

2 Bind the long tail of the wire under and over the tiara four times. Thread on a bead to sit on top of the tiara. Bind the tiara four more times. Hold the tail upwards and thread on one bead 2cm (3/4in) above the tiara. Bend the tail downwards. Twist the wires together until you reach the tiara. Repeat Steps 2 and 3 of **making a bunch of twisted stem beads** on p.34 using the same length of wire.

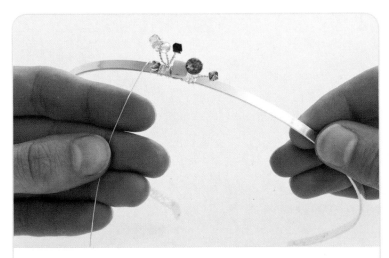

3 Bind the tiara four more times. Continue the sequence of adding beads, binding the tiara, and making twisted stem beads as you work outwards from the centre of the tiara.

4 If you need to finish a length of wire and add a new length, follow Step 3 of **binding with wire and beads** on p.35. Continue making twisted stem beads and binding with beads for 8.5cm (3 3/8in).

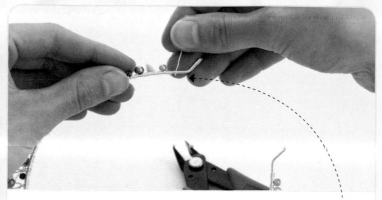

5 Snip a 150cm (60in) length of wire. Follow **binding with wire and beads** on p.35 to bind and bead the tiara, finishing 2cm (¾in) from the end of the tiara. To finish, follow **finishing a straight edge binding** on p.35. Decorate the second half of the tiara to match, starting by binding the short tail of the wire around the centre of the tiara.

Cold enamelling TECHNIQUES

No special equipment is needed for cold enamelling, yet with just the addition of a hardener, the enamels set rock hard with an attractive glossy sheen. There is a large range of enamel colours, which can be mixed to create new shades. Apply the enamels to metal jewellery bezels or blanks. Interesting effects can be achieved by swirling contrast-coloured enamels on a background colour or by applying glitter for extra sparkle.

Mixing colours

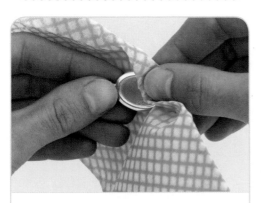

If you wish to mix your own colours, do so before adding hardener. Pour the enamel colours or drop them with a mixing stick or cocktail stick into a mixing cup. Mix the colours evenly with the stick.

Adding hardener

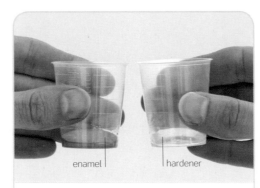

1 The enamel must be mixed accurately – two-parts of enamel colour to one-part of hardener. Pour two-parts of colour into a mixing cup. Pour one-part of hardener into another mixing cup.

2 Pour the hardener into the colour and mix. Leave to stand for 10 minutes to ensure there are no air bubbles. The mixture will remain workable for one hour. Prepare a second colour at the same time if wanted.

Cleaning metal

While the colour is standing, clean the bezel or blank with white spirit on a soft cloth. This degreases the surface.

Applying cold enamel

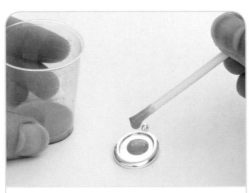

1 With the bezel or blank on a flat surface, apply the enamel to the recess with a mixing stick or cocktail stick.

2 Distribute the enamel up to the outer edges, butting it against the frame of the bezel. Set aside for 24 hours.

Keeping a bezel level

plastic clay support

Often a bezel cannot be kept flat when applying the enamel and while it cures, such as on a ring for example. To keep the bezel level, support it on plastic clay.

Applying a second colour enamel

1 If a second prepared colour is applied immediately after its standing time on top of the first, it will spread on the surface. Apply the colour with a cocktail stick and swirl to distribute it.

2 Alternatively, leave the second colour to stand for a further 10 minutes, then apply it. You will not be able to spread it so much.

Applying enamel in relief

Apply a background colour and leave to dry for 24 hours. Use a cocktail stick to apply other colours in dots or swirls to the background colour. The other colours will stand proud of the surface. Set aside for 24 hours.

Applying glitter

1 Apply a background colour to a bezel and leave to dry for two hours. With the bezel on scrap paper, sprinkle fine glitter onto the background colour. Do not shake off the excess glitter. Set aside for 24 hours without touching.

2 Mix clear cold enamel with hardener (see **adding hardener,** opposite). Apply the clear enamel on top, completely covering the background colour and the glitter. Set aside for 24 hours.

Linked bracelet PROJECT

This charming bracelet is simple to make and is a great introductory project to cold enamelling. The enamelling is applied to bezels that have a loop at each side. These are linked together with figure-of-eight connectors. This bracelet has five bezels and is approximately 18cm (7in) in length. To shorten the bracelet, use fewer bezels; to lengthen it, add more bezels or link extra jump rings at one end.

YOU WILL NEED

- light blue and mint green cold enamel colours
- 3 mixing cups
- cold enamel hardener
- mixing sticks (optional)
- cocktail sticks
- 5 silver 3cm (1¼in) oval bezels with a link at each side
- white spirit
- soft cloth
- 6 silver figure-of-eight connectors
- snipe-nose pliers
- round-nose pliers
- 2 silver jump rings
- silver ring and bar fastening

1 Prepare light blue and mint green cold enamel colours with hardener following **adding hardener** on p.40. While the colours stand, clean the bezels with white spirit on a soft cloth. Apply the light blue colour to the recesses of the bezels with a mixing stick or cocktail stick.

2 Set the bezels and mint green enamel aside for 10 minutes. Using a cocktail stick, swirl a circle of the mint green colour on the light blue background colour. Set aside to cure for 24 hours.

3 With the bezel face down, slip one loop of a figure-of-eight connector through one loop of the bezel. Squeeze the loop of the connector closed with snipe-nose pliers. Attach the other loop of the connector to another bezel. Repeat to link all the bezels.

4 Fix a figure-of-eight connector through the end loops of the first and last bezels and close with snipe-nose pliers. Slip a jump ring through the end loop of the first connector.

5 Slip the loop of the bar of the fastening onto the jump ring. Close the jump ring using two pairs of pliers. Repeat to fix a jump ring to the end loop of the last connector and the ring of the fastening to that jump ring.

Loom weaving TECHNIQUES

Loom-woven beads produce a flat band of beads. You'll need one warp thread more than the number of beads in a row. Create designs by following beading charts drawn on graph paper, with each square representing a bead. Sew the weaving to a band of soft leather or imitation leather to make into a cuff or choker, and fasten with ribbon, or see pp.46–47 for how to make a toggle fastening.

Preparing the loom

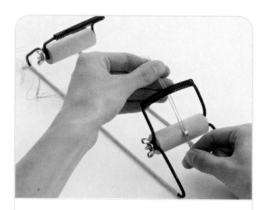

1 Cut warp threads at least 30cm (12in) longer than the intended length of the weaving. Knot the threads together at one end. Divide the bundle in half and slip the knot under the nail on one of the rollers.

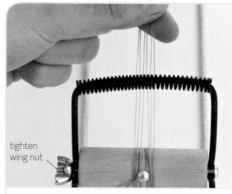

tighten wing nut

2 With the threads taut, turn the roller until they extend 15cm (6in) beyond the second roller. Tighten the wing nut to hold the roller in place. Place one thread in each groove of the spring.

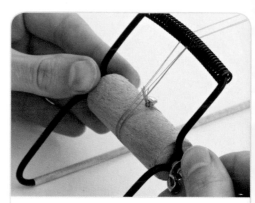

3 Knot the other ends of the warp threads and slip the knot under the nail on the second roller. Loosen the wing nut of this roller and wind the roller to take up the slack. Tighten the wing nut.

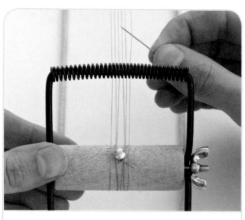

4 Sit the threads in the grooves of the second roller, separating the threads with a needle. Tighten the tension again if necessary by loosening the wing nut, turning the second roller, and tightening the wing nut again. The threads should be taut.

Loom weaving

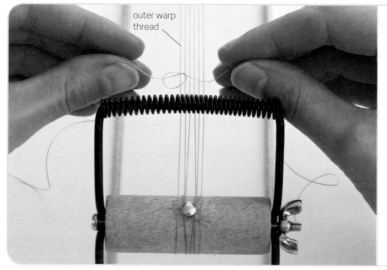

outer warp thread

1 Thread a long length of thread onto a long beading needle: this will be the weft thread. Tie the weft thread to one outer warp thread close to the second roller, leaving a trailing end 15cm (6in) long.

2 Using the beading needle, thread on beads for the first row. Refer to a chart if beading a specific design. There are six warp threads here, so thread on five beads.

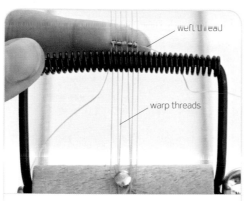

weft thread

warp threads

3 Slip the beads along the weft thread, position the thread at right angles under the warp threads, then press the beads up between the warp threads with a finger.

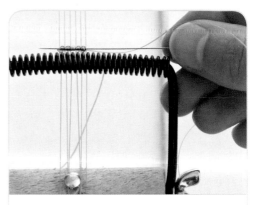

4 To secure the first row, take the needle back through the beads, making sure that it passes above the warp threads. Pick up the next row of beads and repeat.

Adding a new weft thread

When the weft thread starts to run out, weave it back through a few rows of beads. Tie a new long weft thread to an outer warp thread, leaving a 15cm (6in) trailing end. Continue adding beads and weaving as before.

Reaching the first roller

When you reach the first roller, loosen the tension on both rollers. Roll the weaving onto the first roller, tighten the tension, and continue weaving until the weaving is the required length.

Finishing the sides and ends

1 Loosen the tension on the rollers and remove the work. Weave the trailing ends of the weft threads back into the work by inserting the thread on a needle in and out of a few rows of beads. Cut off the excess threads close to the weaving.

2 With a short beading needle, weave each warp thread back through the work, weaving them over and under the weft threads. Cut off the excess threads close to the weaving.

Loom-woven cuff PROJECT

Make this pretty cuff of loom-woven beads in colours to match a favourite outfit. The cuff closes with a pair of toggle and loop fastenings. Bead the subtle pattern of diagonal stripes by following the easy-to-use beading chart on p.92. The cuff measures 18cm (7in) in length. To lengthen or shorten it, add or decrease rows of beads at each end of the chart.

YOU WILL NEED

- loom
- lilac Nymo thread
- scissors
- 10g (⅓oz) lilac seed beads or size 15 Delica beads
- 4g (⅕oz) green seed beads or size 15 Delica beads
- 10g (⅓oz) purple seed beads or size 15 Delica beads
- long beading needle
- short beading needle
- 2 x 8mm (⁵⁄₁₆in) lilac beads

1 Follow **preparing the loom** on p.44, using 17 x 45cm (18in) lengths of warp threads. Use a 1m (40in) length of weft thread to start weaving the design on p.92, following **loom weaving, adding a new weft thread,** and **reaching the first roller** on pp.44–45. Follow **finishing the sides and ends** on p.45, leaving the third, fourth, thirteenth, and fourteenth warp threads free at each end of the weaving.

2 For the toggle, thread the third and fourth warp threads onto a short beading needle. Thread on two lilac seed beads, one 8mm (⁵⁄₁₆in) bead, and one lilac seed bead. Take the needle back through the 8mm (⁵⁄₁₆in) bead and the two seed beads. Adjust the toggle to sit against the end of the weaving.

3 Separate the two threads. With one of the threads on a short beading needle, insert the needle through the fourth bead from the edge in the last row of weaving, then sew through the toggle again to secure.

4 Take the threaded needle back into the last row of beads in the cuff, weaving it over and under the weft threads. Trim away the excess. Thread the other thread on the needle and insert it through the same bead as in Step 3, but starting from the opposite direction. Weave the thread as before and trim the excess.

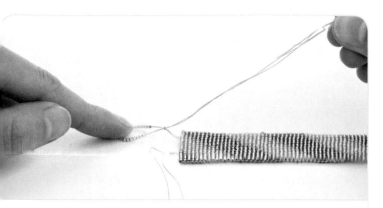 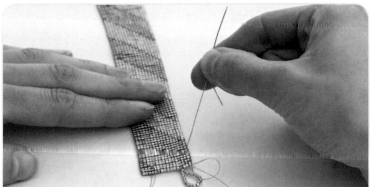

5 Repeat to make a toggle with the thirteenth and fourteenth warp threads. To make a loop at the other end of the cuff, thread the third and fourth threads onto a short beading needle. Thread on 22 lilac seed beads. Insert the needle back through the first seed bead.

6 Adjust the loop to sit against the end of the weaving. Check to see that the loop will slip snugly over the toggle and adjust if needed. Separate the two threads and thread one on a short beading needle. Insert the needle through the fourth bead in the last row of the weaving, then sew through the loop again to secure. Follow Step 4 to secure the threads. Repeat to make a second loop with the thirteenth and fourteenth warp threads.

Polymer clay TECHNIQUES

Polymer clay is a great modelling medium for making beads. Canework or millefiori beads – plain beads covered with thin decorative slices from canes of coloured clay – evoke the look of Venetian glass. To begin, knead the clay a little to produce a soft, pliable clay. Wash your hands regularly while you work to avoid mixing one colour into another.

Blending colours

Twist together logs of clay in different colours. Stretch and twist the clay, double it over, and repeat to create a marbled effect. You can use the clay at this stage or continue blending it to achieve an even colour.

Rolling a clay sheet

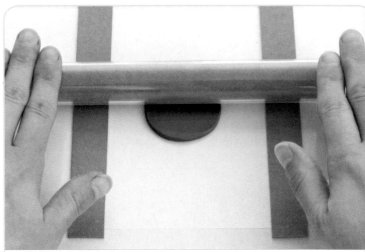

To roll clay to a specific thickness, place it on a non-stick sheet with a strip of card on either side. Roll out using a non-stick roller. Vary the thickness of the card or layer the strips for thinner or thicker sheets of clay.

Making a jelly-roll cane

1 Roll two 1mm (1/16in) thick sheets of different coloured clays. Stack the sheets and cut to a 5cm (2in) square using a tissue blade. Flatten two opposite edges with a non-stick roller.

2 Starting at one flattened edge, roll the layers tightly and evenly. Roll the cane on a flat surface to smooth the join. Cut the ends of the roll level.

Making a flower cane

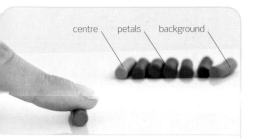

1 Roll eight 6mm (¼in) thick logs – one for the centre, five for the petals, and two for the background. Trim the logs to 3cm (1¼in).

2 Roll a 1mm (¹⁄₁₆in) sheet of a fourth colour for the outer petals. Cut it into five 3 x 2cm (1¼ x ¾in) rectangles and wrap one around each of the petal logs. Roll to smooth the joins, then trim to 3cm (1¼in) long.

3 Arrange the petal logs around the centre log with the outer petals facing outwards. Cut the background logs lengthwise into quarters. Place a quarter between each petal log. Roll the cane a few times to smooth the circumference.

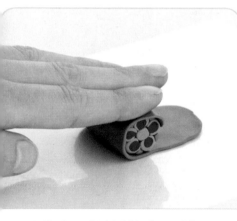

4 Roll a 2mm (¹⁄₁₀in) thick sheet of the background colour and wrap it around the flower. Roll the cane to smooth the join. See below to make pendants or continue to roll the cane to lengthen it. Cut the ends level.

Making plain and canework beads

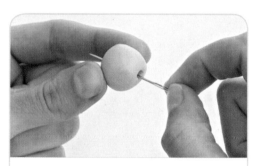

1 Roll a ball of clay and pierce a hole through the centre with a thick needle. Enlarge the hole with the needle and reshape. You can use scrap clay if the bead is to be covered in canework.

2 For canework beads, cut thin slices of jelly-roll cane and press them to the beads, butting the slices together. Fill gaps with tiny bits of matching clay. Roll the beads to smooth them, then re-pierce the hole.

Making pendants

Cut discs of canework 4mm (³⁄₁₆in) thick from a flower cane. Pierce a hole at the top with a thick needle. Bake the pendants flat on a baking sheet following the manufacturer's instructions. After baking, fix a bail through the hole (see p.25).

Baking beads

Thread beads onto a wooden skewer or thick wire for support while baking. Rest the skewer across an ovenproof bowl, then bake in a domestic oven following the manufacturer's instructions.

Polymer clay beads PROJECT

Make this pretty necklace to show off a set of canework beads. The beads are graduated in size and include spotted beads, which are quick and simple to make. Placing small, plain clay "spacer" beads between the larger beads emphasizes each decorative bead and helps them lay in a gentle curve. Of course, you could use glass or metal spacer beads for a change of texture.

YOU WILL NEED

- non-stick sheet
- light grey, dark blue, turquoise, and mid-blue clay, plus scraps of any colour
- 2 strips of 2mm ($^1/_{10}$in) thick card
- non-stick roller
- tissue blade
- thick needle
- wooden skewer or thick wire for baking
- 80cm (32in) flexible beading wire
- masking tape
- 2 silver crimps
- 2 silver jump rings
- crimping or snipe-nose pliers
- necklace fastening

1 Working on a non-stick sheet, blend a 3.5cm (1$^3/_8$in) ball of light grey and a 1.5cm ($^5/_8$in) ball of dark blue clay to achieve a mid-grey clay. Blend a 2cm ($^3/_4$in) ball each of light grey and turquoise clay to make a light turquoise clay.

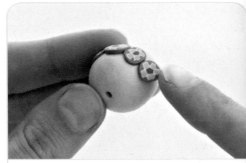

2 Follow **making a flower cane** on p.49 to make a flower cane with a dark blue centre, light turquoise petals, light grey outer petals, and mid-blue background. Roll to 8mm ($^5/_{16}$in) thick. Make a plain 2cm ($^3/_4$in) bead using scrap clay and pierce a hole through the centre with a thick needle. Press flower cane slices in a row around the middle of the bead.

3 Follow **making a jelly-roll cane** on p.48 to make a jelly-roll cane with light grey clay inside and mid-blue clay outside. Cut a 4cm (1$^1/_2$in) length of the cane and roll to 6mm ($^1/_4$in) thick. Roll the remaining cane to 8mm ($^5/_{16}$in) thick. Cut slices from the smaller cane and press to the bead above and below the flowers. Roll the bead to smooth it, then re-pierce the hole.

4 From scrap clay, roll four 2cm ($^3/_4$in) beads, four 1.5cm ($^5/_8$in) beads, and four 1.2cm ($^1/_2$in) beads. Apply flower cane slices to two beads of each size and 8mm ($^5/_{16}$in) jelly-roll cane slices to the remaining beads.

5 To make the spotted beads, roll four 1.5cm ($^5/_8$in), four 1.2cm ($^1/_2$in), and four 1cm ($^3/_8$in) balls of mid-blue clay. Pierce holes through the beads with the needle. Roll a 1mm ($^1/_{16}$in) thick log of light grey clay, cut it into slices, and press to the mid-blue beads. Roll the beads to embed the spots then re-pierce the holes. Now make twenty-six 6mm ($^1/_4$in) light grey spacer beads.

6 Follow **baking beads** on p.49, then thread the beads onto flexible beading wire. Graduate outwards in size from the centre, with the largest bead at the centre and a spacer bead between each decorated bead. Follow **attaching a crimp** on p.26 and **attaching a necklace fastening** on p.27 to complete the necklace.

Air-dry clay TECHNIQUES

Some air-dry clays are in two parts – the clay and a hardener – which helps the clay dry rock hard. If you want to blend the colours to produce the exact shade you want, do so after mixing in the hardener. Then break off the amount of clay needed and store the rest in an airtight container. Be aware that some air-dry clays shrink as they dry.

Using two-part clay

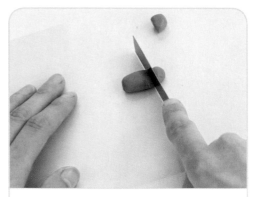

If your clay is in two parts, cut off equal amounts of each and knead together until blended, following the manufacturer's instructions. One part might be shinier than the other; once mixed, there should be no shiny streaks running through the clay.

Blending colours

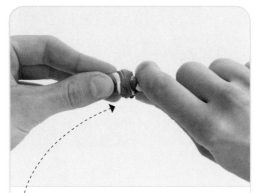

Blend colours after mixing a two-part clay. Twist together different coloured logs of clay, stretching, twisting, and doubling them over to achieve an evenly mixed shade. Keep any mixed leftover clay wrapped in clingfilm in an airtight container until needed.

Rolling a clay sheet

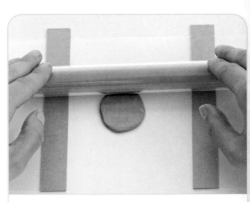

Place the clay on a non-stick sheet between two strips of card. To stop the clay sticking, sprinkle talcum powder on a non-stick roller. Roll the clay. If you need to vary its thickness, use thicker or thinner strips of cards.

Using a template

1 Cut out the template from baking paper and place it on the rolled-out clay. Cut around the template using a craft knife, then remove the template.

2 Peel away the excess clay and store it wrapped in clingfilm in an airtight container so that it doesn't dry out.

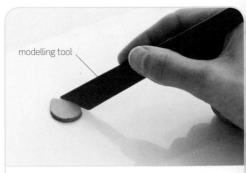

modelling tool

3 Pat the cut edges of the shape with a straight-sided clay modelling tool to neaten the edges. With the blade flat against the surface, slip a tissue blade or the blade of a craft knife under the clay to lift it.

Using a metal cutter

Press the cutter firmly onto the rolled-out clay. Peel away the excess clay and store it wrapped in clingfilm in an airtight container. Remove the cutter and slip a tissue blade or the blade of a craft knife under the shape to lift it.

Making a small hole

With the clay lying flat, insert a thick needle through the clay to make a hole. To do the same on a three-dimensional piece, hold the piece carefully and pierce a hole through the clay with a thick needle.

Using a bezel

Choose a clay that will not shrink and use a bezel with a rim that overhangs the recess. Press the clay onto the centre of the bezel, then smooth it outwards with your thumb to fit under the rim of the bezel.

Using jewellery stones and chatons

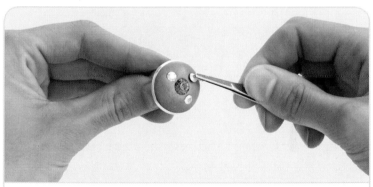

Place a jewellery stone or chaton on the clay using tweezers or a moistened fingertip. If necessary, gently nudge the stone into position with tweezers. Press the stone into the clay with the tips of the tweezers.

Forming three-dimensional shapes

For a three-dimensional shape, place the clay over a suitably shaped item, such as a drinking straw or a teaspoon for a curved shape. Alternatively, rest the clay on a scrunched-up piece of clingfilm.

Drying air-dry clay

To dry the clay to a hard, durable finish, follow the manufacturer's instructions and set it aside, usually for about 24 hours. If necessary, the hardened clay can be gently smoothed by sanding with fine sandpaper or a needle file.

Air-dry clay pendant PROJECT

Make a cascade of delicate blooms from air-dry clay to hang as pendants from a long necklace. Each flower has a cluster of sparkling crystal chatons at the centre and hangs on headpins between silver and crystal beads. For best results, make the flowers in batches of three at a time so that your clay is easy to work with and does not dry out.

YOU WILL NEED

- baking paper
- pencil
- scissors
- 20g (³⁄₄oz) each of white and amethyst air-dry clay
- craft knife
- clingfilm
- non-stick sheet
- strips of 1mm (¹⁄₁₆in) thick card
- talcum powder
- non-stick roller
- straight-sided clay modelling tool
- round-ended clay modelling tool
- 18 x 1mm (¹⁄₁₆in) light amethyst chatons
- tweezers
- thick needle
- 5cm (2in) silver headpin
- 2 x 2.5cm (1in) silver headpins
- wire cutters
- round-nose pliers
- glue
- 90cm (35in) flexible beading wire
- 32 x 4mm (³⁄₁₆in) light amethyst bicone crystal beads
- 260 silver rocaille beads
- 2 silver crimps
- 2 jump rings
- crimping or snipe-nose pliers
- necklace fastening

1 Trace the flower template on p.92 onto baking paper and cut it out. If using a two-part clay, mix the two halves following **using two-part clay** on p.52. Blend a 1.5cm (⁵⁄₈in) ball of white clay and a 1cm (³⁄₈in) ball of amethyst clay to make a pale amethyst shade. Divide the clay into three equal pieces. Wrap two pieces in clingfilm.

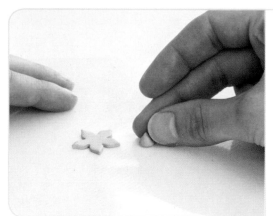

2 Roll the third piece of clay out to 1mm (¹⁄₁₆in) thick, following **rolling a clay sheet** on p.52. Use the template to cut one clay flower. Pull away the excess clay. Remove the paper template, pat the edges to smooth the clay with the straight-sided clay modelling tool. Roll a 5mm (¹⁄₄in) ball of clay using some of the excess clay from the flower, then squeeze the ball into a cone shape. Wrap any leftover clay in clingfilm.

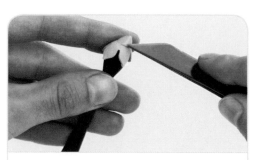

3 Lift the flower by slipping the blade of a craft knife underneath it. Smooth the flower over the rounded end of the round-ended clay modelling tool. Press the cone on top. Smooth the cone onto the flower with the straight-sided clay modelling tool to hide the join.

4 Lift the flower off the tool and splay the petals open. Holding the flower between your fingers, place three chatons on the flower centre and gently press them into the clay with the tips of a pair of tweezers.

5 Pierce a hole through the cone with a thick needle. Use the two pieces of clay set aside in Step 1 to make two more flower pendants, then repeat the steps with a fresh piece of clay to make three more. Set the pieces aside to harden. Follow **making a single loop** on p.24 to fix four flowers on a 5cm (2in) headpin and each of the two remaining flowers on 2.5cm (1in) headpins.

6 Thread the long headpin, three crystal beads, one short headpin, then a sequence of one crystal bead and 10 silver rocaille beads 13 times onto flexible beading wire. Repeat on the other half of the necklace. Follow **attaching a crimp** on p.26 and **attaching a necklace fastening** on p.27 to finish.

Metal clay TECHNIQUES

Metal clay is a fabulous material that looks uninspiring to begin with but once fired, becomes a beautiful precious metal. The clay is made from fine particles of pure metal mixed with organic binders and water. The clay can be fired on a gas hob or with a gas torch, making it suitable for home use, or it can be fired in a kiln.

Preparing metal clay

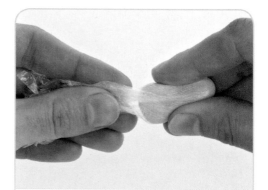

Only break off enough clay for your needs and keep the rest wrapped in clingfilm and sealed in an airtight container. Wrap the clay you are using in clingfilm and knead for a few seconds to soften it.

Rolling metal clay

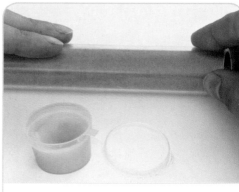

1 Smooth badger balm or olive oil sparingly onto a non-stick roller to stop it sticking.

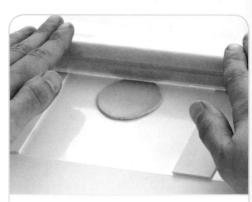

2 Place the clay on a non-stick surface with a strip of card at least 2mm (¹⁄₁₀in) thick on either side. Roll the clay, resting the ends of the roller on the card strips.

Adding texture

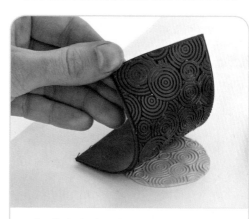

Rub a little badger balm or olive oil on a rubber stamp or texture mat, then press it firmly and evenly onto the clay to make an imprint. Lift off the stamp or mat.

Using a cutter

1 Smooth badger balm or olive oil sparingly onto a metal cutter. Press the cutter firmly onto the clay. Pull away the excess clay, then lift the cutter.

2 Wrap excess clay immediately in clingfilm and store it in an airtight container. Pat the edges of the cut shape with a flat-sided clay modelling tool to neaten them.

Making a hole

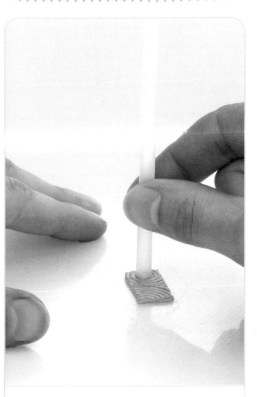

The clay will shrink by 8 to 10 per cent after firing, so make the hole large enough to accommodate whatever will be inserted through it. Pierce the clay with a drinking straw or with a thick needle.

Sanding the clay

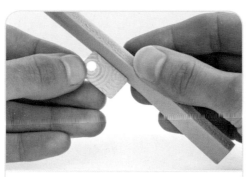

1 Leave the piece to dry for a few days. Handle the clay gently as it is brittle, and sand any rough edges with a sanding pad.

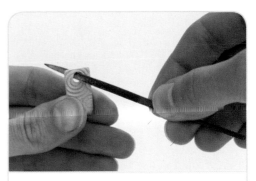

2 Use a needle file to even out or enlarge holes. The piece can be sanded once fired but it is easier to do so now.

Firing on a gas hob

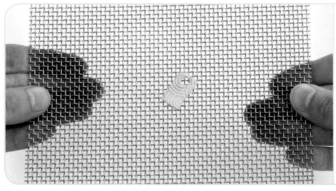

Place the clay on a sheet of stainless-steel mesh. Place the mesh on a gas burner and turn the heat on fully – the clay will smoke for a few seconds. Heat for 10 minutes, then turn off the gas and leave the clay to cool.

Polishing the metal

1 After firing, brush with a soft brass brush for a satin finish. For a mirror finish, polish with dampened coarse polishing paper, then with dampened fine polishing paper.

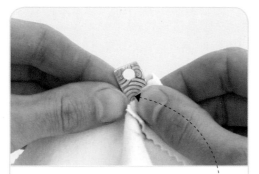

2 Give a final polish with a polishing cloth; this will highlight any raised areas. Burnishing with a metal crochet hook or the back of a teaspoon will also produce a shine.

FIRING SAFETY NOTE

Always refer to the clay manufacturer's firing instructions. Pieces no larger than 3cm (1¼in) in diameter can be fired on a gas hob. The clay must be bone dry before firing or it could "pop" and burst. For safety, place a stainless-steel mesh cage over the clay when firing.

The clay can also be fired with a butane gas torch or in a kiln. To fire with a gas torch, place the completely dry clay on a ceramic fibre brick, which in turn is placed on a fireproof surface. Direct the flame at a 45° angle, 5cm (2in) away from the clay. Move the flame around the piece and fire, following the clay manufacturer's instructions.

Metal clay brooch PROJECT

This charming bird brooch is 99.9 per cent silver and would make a delightful gift, although you may decide to keep it for yourself! The bird has a satin finish, while its wing is highly polished to a mirror shine. The simple decoration is created with humble dressmaking pins. As a finishing touch, beaded ballpins are suspended below the bird like a pair of whimsical "legs".

YOU WILL NEED

- baking paper
- pencil
- scissors
- 12g (½oz) silver metal clay
- non-stick sheet
- 2 strips of 2mm (¹⁄₁₀in) thick card
- badger balm or olive oil
- non-stick roller
- craft knife
- clingfilm
- medium artist's paintbrush
- jar of water
- thick needle
- flat-sided clay modelling tool
- plain dressmaking pin

- glass-headed pin
- fine sandpaper
- needle file
- sheet of stainless-steel mesh
- soft brass brush
- polishing papers
- polishing cloth
- 2 x 3.5cm (1³⁄₈in) sterling-silver ballpins
- 2 x 5mm (¹⁄₄in) blue beads
- 2 x 4mm (³⁄₁₆in) sterling-silver rice beads
- round-nose pliers
- brooch pin
- epoxy resin glue

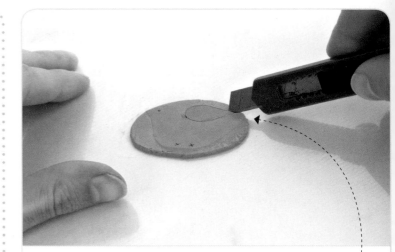

1 Trace the wing and bird templates on p.92 onto baking paper and cut out. Follow **preparing metal clay** and **rolling metal clay** on p.56, rolling the clay 2mm (¹⁄₁₀in) thick. Place the templates on the clay and cut around them with a craft knife. Peel off the templates. Lift off the excess clay and store it wrapped in clingfilm in an airtight container.

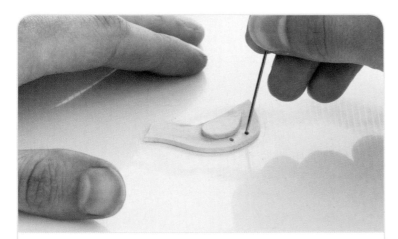

2 Lift the wing by slipping the craft knife underneath it. Moisten the underside with water. Position the wing on the bird. Referring to the template, pierce two holes at the crosses with a thick needle. Wiggle the needle to enlarge the holes, remembering that the clay will shrink when fired.

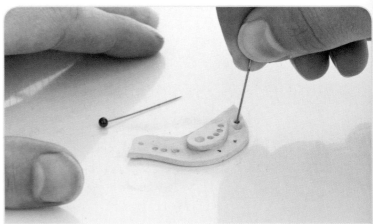

3 Pat the edges of the bird with the flat-sided clay modelling tool. Use the head of a dressmaking pin to make the bird's eye. To add other decorations, press the head of a glass-headed pin into the body and wing, then the head of a dressmaking pin.

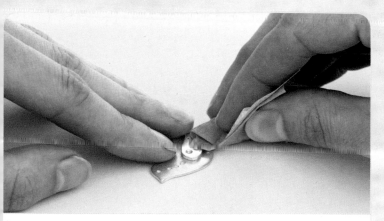

4 Follow **sanding the clay** and **firing on a gas hob** on p.57. Polish both sides of the bird with a soft brass brush. Polish the wing with dampened polishing paper, starting with a coarse paper and finishing with a fine paper. Carefully give the wing a final polish with a polishing cloth.

5 Follow **making a single loop** on p.24 to fix a blue bead and a silver rice bead onto both silver ballpins. Open the loop of one ballpin and slip it through one hole on the bird. Close the loop with round-nose pliers. Repeat to fix the second ballpin. Follow the glue manufacturer's instructions to stick a brooch pin to the back of the bird.

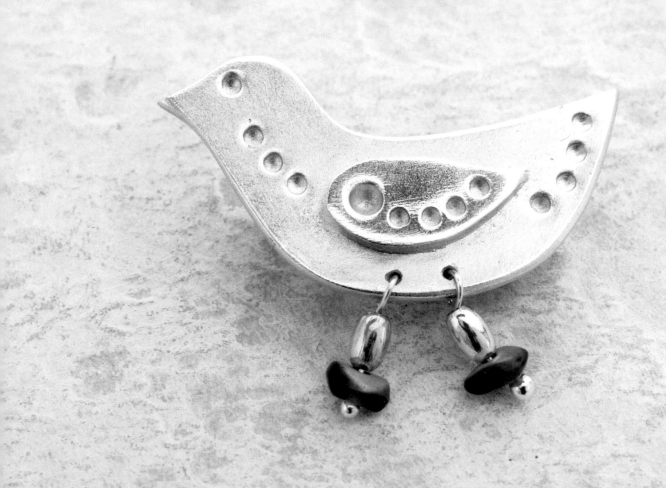

Metal clay pendant PROJECT

This designer leaf pendant looks delicate and expensive, but is easy to make yourself at a fraction of the price of a shop-bought pendant. Made using a real leaf, use the template on p.92 or adapt it to a leaf shape of your own. If your clay dries out, rehydrate it with water.

YOU WILL NEED

- cooking spray oil
- baking paper
- small rolling pin
- playing cards
- 7g silver clay
- leaves or leaf skeletons
- craft knife
- small straw
- wet and dry sandpaper (600 grit)/sanding pad (220 grit)
- heatproof tile
- kitchen blow torch

- tweezers
- soft wire brush
- metal spoon
- 2 pairs of pliers
- jump ring
- jewellery chain

1 Spray a little oil over the baking paper, the rolling pin, and your hands to prevent the clay sticking. Place two stacks of playing cards (4 cards in each stack) about 5cm (2in) apart on your baking paper as rolling guides. Gently knead the clay and place it between the stacks of cards. Roll it out.

2 Lift up the clay and place a leaf or skeleton leaf underneath, then put another on top. With your cards still in place, roll over the clay again to transfer the imprint to both sides.

3 Peel away the leaves and cut around the template outline on p.92. Using the straw, make a hole in the leaf about 5mm (⅕in) from the top and big enough for your jump ring to move freely. Roll up any scraps of clay and store them in clingfilm in an airtight container.

4 Leave the clay to dry overnight. Using a small piece of sandpaper, carefully smooth the edges of your leaf – it will be fragile at this stage.

5 Place your leaf on a ceramic tile. Hold your torch about 5cm (2in) from the item to be fired. Move the flame around evenly. The leaf will start to glow – you need to maintain this for 2 minutes. Let the item cool on the tile, or carefully lift it with tweezers and place it in cold water.

6 Once cold, the leaf will be matt white. Gently brush it with a soft wire brush to reveal its silver colour. Achieve a high shine by rubbing it with the back of a metal spoon. Using two pairs of pliers, gently twist the ends of the jump ring away from each other. Thread it through the hole in your leaf and twist to close. Thread the pendant onto the chain.

Film and leadwork TECHNIQUES

Using a combination of coloured, self-adhesive film and self-adhesive lead on clear glass panels – to hang in a window – or objects, this technique creates a beautiful stained-glass effect without the need for specialist equipment. The film comes in myriad colours and the lead strips in different widths and profiles so the possibilities are endless.

Cleaning the glass

Drawing and colouring the design

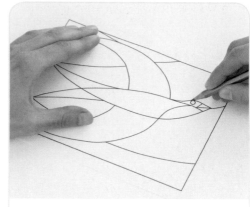

Wipe the glass with methylated spirit to remove any grease, fingerprints, or smudges from the surface. Wash the glass in warm soapy water, rinse, and dry thoroughly.

1 Mark the size of your glass panel on a piece of paper. Draw your design to comfortably fit within this size. Make a duplicate design to use later (see below).

2 Colour up your design; you may want to try out several colourways before choosing the best one. Trim your paper to the size of the design.

Cutting out the pieces of film

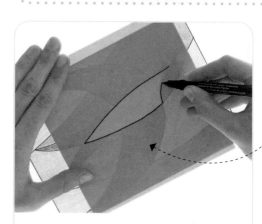

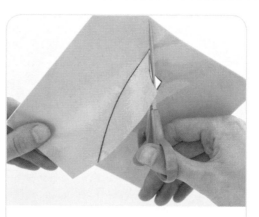

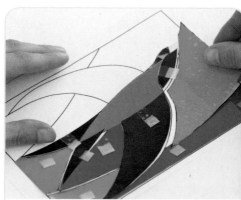

1 Gather together the sheets of coloured film. Hold the design up to a window with the first sheet of film on top. Trace the area with a fine permanent pen.

2 Put the design down and pick up some small sharp scissors. Cut out the film, following the drawn line. Now repeat for all the differently coloured areas of the design.

3 Arrange the pieces of film on a duplicate design to ensure you cut out every piece of film needed. Once all pieces are cut, you can start to apply them in turn.

Applying the coloured film

1 Fix the design to the back of the glass using Blu Tack, so that you see the design all the time. Take the first cut-out piece of film and carefully peel off the backing sheet.

2 Working from one edge, slowly position the film on the glass and, using a sponge, press the film down and ease out any air bubbles; the side of a thumb works well, too.

3 Now repeat with the other pieces of coloured film until the design is completed.

Cutting and applying the lead strip

1 Cut the self-adhesive lead strip a bit longer than you need, using scissors. Lay it on the design and mark where to cut.

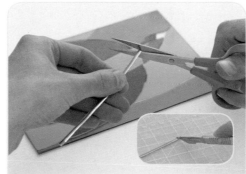

2 Cut the strip at the mark at the correct angle for the line on the design, using scissors or a craft knife and cutting board.

3 Peel the backing sheet from the lead strip, a little at a time. Then stick down the strip along the line of the design.

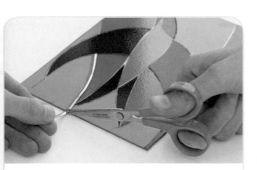

4 Trim the lead strip at the edge of the glass panel. Continue laying down the lead strips until the design is complete.

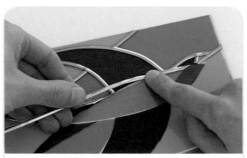

5 When a strip of lead joins another, cut it at an angle. Ensure the final strips cover the joins and ends for a neat finish.

6 Press down firmly along all of the strips to ensure a firm bond between the glass and the lead. Wash your hands thoroughly.

Film and leadwork vase PROJECT

A plain vase has been transformed with the addition of a colourful, patterned band of film and leadwork. On a bright windowsill, the light will shine through the various square and rectangular panels of this Mondrian-esque design to bring whatever colours you choose to use to full effect. Such colourful bands would also work well on cylindrical vases or glass picture frames.

YOU WILL NEED

- 1 rectangular glass vase
- 2 sheets of paper
- pencil and some coloured pencils
- ruler
- scissors
- sticky tape
- sheets of self-adhesive coloured film
- Blu Tack
- a roll of 3mm ($1/8$in) oval profile self-adhesive lead

1 After cleaning the vase (see p.62), cut a piece of paper that fits all the way around the inside of the vase. Draw out and colour in your design and make a duplicate. Trace onto the sheets of coloured film, as necessary, using a fine permanent pen.

2 Cut out the pieces of coloured film. As you go, start to stick these pieces down carefully onto one of the paper designs with sticky tape. Pieces that wrap around a corner will need to be longer than the paper design to account for the glass' thickness.

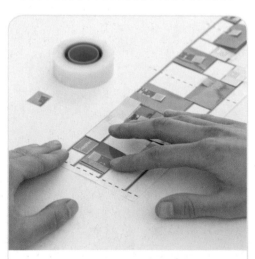

3 Once you've cut out all the coloured film pieces, finish sticking them to the duplicate design to check that you've got all the shapes you need.

4 Fix the paper design inside the vase with Blu Tack. Stick on the coloured film pieces one at a time, taking them from the paper design in turn.

backing sheet

5 Cut small lead strips for the short lengths, peel off the backing sheet, and fix down to match the design. Work around the vase until all strips are done.

the top and bottom strips of lead are added last

6 Cut two long lead strips to form the borders of the band. Peel off the backing, wrap around, and cut to length. Press down firmly and wash your hands.

Painting glass TECHNIQUES

Glass painting is an inexpensive craft that requires minimal tools and materials. It is a great way to recycle old glassware and give it a new lease of life. Clear glass is the most versatile for painting on, but also consider coloured and frosted glass. Glass paint applied to frosted glass will make it transparent. Practise painting on acetate or an old piece of glass before starting on a project.

Making a template for a straight-sided or conical container

1 Slip a piece of tracing paper inside a straight-sided or conical container. Adjust the paper so that it rests against the glass, then tape it in place. Mark the position of the overlap and the upper edge with a pencil.

2 Remove the tracing paper and cut out the template along the overlap and upper edge. Transfer your design onto the tracing paper with a black pen. Stick the tracing under the glass with masking tape, butting the side edges of the template together.

Sticking a template under a double curvature

1 Templates to be used on rounded glassware need to be adapted to fit the shape. Make cuts into the template with a pair of scissors.

2 Tape the template under the glass at the top and bottom. The cuts will overlap or spread open to fit the curves of the glassware.

Transferring a design

1 If the aperture is too small to stick a template inside, the design can be transferred to the outer surface of the glass with a Chinagraph pencil. Turn the tracing over and redraw the lines with a Chinagraph pencil.

2 Tape the template, Chinagraph-pencil-side down, on the glass. Draw over the lines again with a sharp HB pencil to transfer the design onto the glass. Remove the template.

Applying outliner

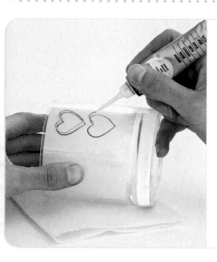

1 Resting the piece on kitchen paper and with the template in place, squeeze the tube of outliner, gently drawing it along the outline of the design. Leave to dry then turn the piece to continue

2 Wipe away major mistakes immediately with kitchen paper. When dry, neaten any blobs with a craft knife. Once painted, the viewer's eye will be drawn to the painted areas and not the outliner, so don't overdo the neatening.

Painting on glass

1 Resting the piece on kitchen paper, apply the glass paint generously with a medium paintbrush. Use a fine paintbrush to push the paint into any corners. If working on a curve, keep the glass steady to avoid the paint running to one side.

2 To blend one colour into another, apply both colours to the glass, then mix them together where they meet, making sure that the paint reaches the edge of the outliner. Leave to dry, then turn the glass to continue painting.

Tea light holder PROJECT

Make a set of pretty painted tea light holders in warm shades of red and orange, outlined in gold. Candlelight will enhance the painted blossoms as it shines through the transparent glass paint. Use the simple motifs in different combinations to give individuality to a set of tea light holders. For a delicate finishing touch, decorate the motifs with tiny dots applied with outliner.

YOU WILL NEED

- straight-sided clear glass tea light holder
- tracing paper
- scissors
- pencil
- ruler
- black felt-tip pen
- masking tape
- kitchen paper
- gold outliner
- piece of white paper
- orange, red, and yellow transparent glass paints
- medium and fine artist's paintbrushes

1 Make a template and divide it into fifths. Trace the blossom and leaf motif on p.92 onto each section 6mm (¼in) below the upper edge with the felt-tip pen. Tape the template inside the tea light holder with masking tape.

2 Resting the tea light holder on its side on kitchen paper, trace the uppermost motif with gold outliner. Leave to dry. Turn the tea light holder and repeat to outline all the motifs. Remove the template when the outliner has dried.

3 Slip a piece of white paper inside the tea light holder to show up the area being painted. Apply orange paint to the outer edge of the petals with a medium paintbrush. Apply red paint to the inner edge with a fine paintbrush. Blend the colours at the centre. Leave to dry. Clean the paintbrushes.

4 Apply yellow paint to the pointed end of a leaf with a clean fine paintbrush. Apply orange paint to the rounded end with a medium paintbrush. Blend the colours at the centre of the leaf. Leave to dry then turn the glass and continue painting.

5 When the last motif is dry, apply a dot of gold outliner at the centre of the flower to neaten it. Apply three tiny dots along the centre of the petals, then five dots along the leaf. Repeat on all the motifs. Leave the outliner to dry.

Painting china TECHNIQUES

Working with ceramic paints is as close as you can get to colour glazing ceramics without having to invest in expensive equipment, such as a kiln, to fire and set the colour. Ceramic paints come in a vast selection of colours and are easy and safe to use. Paint onto your chosen piece of china and bake in the oven to heat-fix.

Priming the surface

Use a cloth dipped in white spirit to clean the ceramic surface so that it is grease-free and ready to work on. Leave to dry.

Sketching and transferring your design

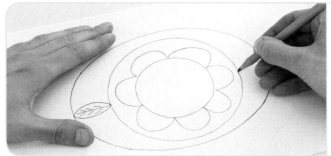

1 Sketch out your ideas on paper: it's a good idea to trace around the outline of your receptacle first to establish the frame within which your design must fit.

2 Once you are happy with your design, transfer it onto the ceramic. Since it is difficult to mark a glazed surface with pencil, transfer the design using a fine paintbrush and ceramic paints, then wash or wipe off any mistakes.

Experimenting with colour

Use a plain white tile for mixing different colour combinations and experimenting with paint effects (think of the tile as an artist's palette). Adding white to a colour makes it look more solid and less opaque.

Achieving different effects with paintbrushes

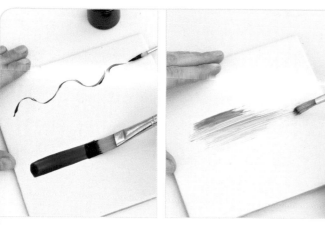

Different brushes give different results: a soft-haired brush produces soft, delicate paint marks, whereas a coarse paintbrush gives a streaky effect. Use different width brushes to produce thinner or thicker lines.

Rinsing paintbrushes

Rinse paintbrushes in cold water as soon as possible after use.

Sponging

1 Pour a little ceramic paint into a shallow dish or onto a tile (rather than dip the sponge directly into the paint pot).

dry make-up sponge

2 Dip a dry make-up sponge into the paint and dab it onto the surface. You can build up stronger colour by leaving the paint to dry then sponging on another layer of colour. Rinse the sponge in cold water after use.

Achieving a sgraffito effect

This is a painting technique where the colour is scratched off to reveal the surface underneath. The term comes from the Italian word "sgraffire", meaning "to scratch". Drag a cocktail stick or the end of a wooden paintbrush handle into wet paint to achieve a scratched effect.

FIXING CERAMIC PAINTS

Once the paint is dry, place the painted ceramic in a cold oven and then set the oven to the recommended temperature. Bake for the stated time, turn off the heat, and leave to cool in the oven. Do not be tempted to remove the ceramic from the oven when it is still hot as the sudden change in temperature may make it crack.

Fruit bowl PROJECT

This simple but effective project transforms a plain white ceramic bowl into a novel fruit bowl that will brighten up any kitchen. The inspiration here is a watermelon, but you could just as easily use an apple, with the outer surface of the bowl painted red or green, the inside cream, and the pips painted in the bottom of the bowl.

YOU WILL NEED

- white ceramic bowl
- cloth
- white spirit
- coarse 1–2cm (⅝in) wide paintbrush
- ceramic paints in peridot green, coral red, and dark brown
- cocktail stick
- shallow dish
- make-up sponge
- ceramic tile
- fine paintbrush

1 Clean the entire surface of the bowl, inside and out, using a cloth dipped in white spirit. Leave to dry before painting the outside of the bowl.

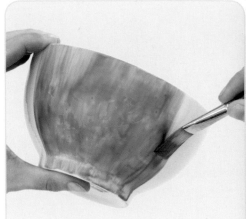

2 Using the coarse paintbrush, apply peridot green using swift, straight strokes. Start at the base of the bowl and work all the way to the rim. Try not to leave any gaps between strokes.

3 Work your way all around the bowl. Turn it upside down and, while the paint is still wet, brush it again with a dry brush to create texture. Work fast as the paint dries quickly but ensure the paint isn't too tacky as it may come off with the second brushing.

4 To create even more texture, add sgraffito work while the paint is still wet. Use a cocktail stick to scratch off lines of paint from the rim to the base of the bowl. Leave to dry for 24 hours.

5 Pour red paint into a dish and dip a dry make-up sponge in the colour. Dab the sponge on a tile to remove excess paint. Start in the centre of the bowl and work up the sides all the way to the rim to meet the green paint, dipping and dabbing the sponge as you go. Leave to dry for 15 minutes.

6 To paint the pips, dip a fine paintbrush in dark brown paint and paint pip-shaped dots inside the bowl. Don't overload the paintbrush or the paint will run. Leave to dry for 24 hours, then bake in the oven following the manufacturer's instructions. Leave to cool completely in the oven before removing.

Dandelion vase PROJECT

A little paint and a creative design transforms a plain vase into the perfect gift for a teacher or friend. Practice applying even dots and smooth lines to paper before applying to china or porcelain, then when you are confident you can position the fly-away dandelion seeds wherever you like. Use the template on p.92 or create your own design.

YOU WILL NEED

- baby wipes or damp cloth
- ceramic vase
- scissors
- red transfer paper
- clear tape
- ballpoint pen
- black food-safe ceramic pen or paint

1 Before you begin, clean the vase using soap and water or a cloth. This is to remove any loose dust or grease from the surface. Photocopy the template from p.92 and enlarge or reduce it to fit your vase.

2 Place transfer paper behind the template, and cut out the main dandelion motif to fit your vase. Cut out the smaller dandelion seeds separately.

3 Position the cut-out dandelion template on the front of the vase, and tape it down with the transfer paper underneath. Position the seeds around the dandelion head, and on one adjoining side. It's best to complete only two sides at a time so that you never have to turn the vase directly on to the transfer paper.

4 Using a ballpoint pen, firmly trace the design on to the vase. Use solid lines across the dots as these show up best. Remove the paper and make sure the lines are visible. If not, wipe off with a baby wipe or damp cloth, cut a new piece of transfer paper and repeat, pressing down more firmly.

5 Use a paint pen or paint in a dispenser to draw the stem of the dandelion in one continuous line. Using the template as a guide, fill in the rest of the lines on the dandelion design with dots. Keep the spacing even and work quickly to avoid the paint pooling. Add short, solid lines to the ends of the dandelion seeds and again fill the lines with dots.

6 Turn to the second side of the vase. Transfer the design and remove the template. Add dots and short, solid lines as before. Let the paint dry, before repeating the process with dandelion seeds on the remaining two sides. When the vase is dry, use a damp cloth to wipe off the transfer lines.

Painting tiles TECHNIQUES

You can buy plain white bathroom or kitchen tiles quite cheaply from hardware stores. Transform them into colourful coasters, trivets, or even a kitchen or bathroom splashback with the help of ceramic paints, which come in a rainbow of delightful colours.

Designing and creating stencils

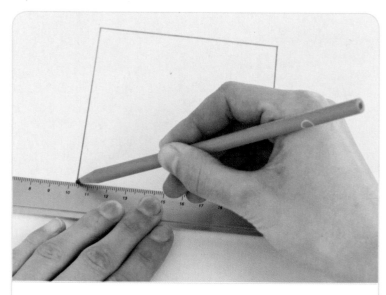

1 Using a pencil and ruler, mark onto card or thick paper the outline of the item you'll be painting onto (in this case, a tile). This outline is the frame within which your design must fit.

2 Draw your design onto the card. Centre the design within the frame and leave enough of an edge around it for the background.

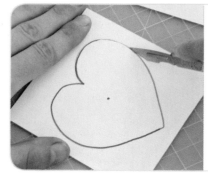

3 Once you're happy with the design, place the card on a cutting mat and use a scalpel to carefully cut around the drawn shape. You'll end up with two stencils: the solid shape you've cut out and its frame.

Fixing the stencil in place

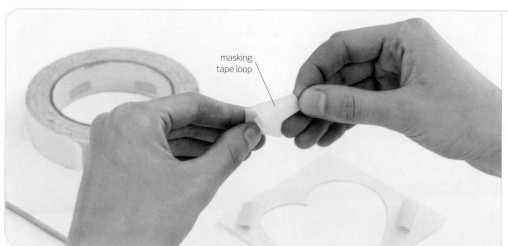

masking tape loop

Use a cloth dipped in white spirit to clean the surface of the tile. Cut a piece of masking tape and make it into a loop. On the reverse side of the frame stencil, stick a loop on each corner. Position the stencil in the centre of the tile and press it down to stick it in place.

Sponging

Using a dry make-up sponge dipped in ceramic paint, apply the colour to the tile. Press the inside edges of the stencil down with your fingers to ensure the paint doesn't seep underneath.

Removing the stencil

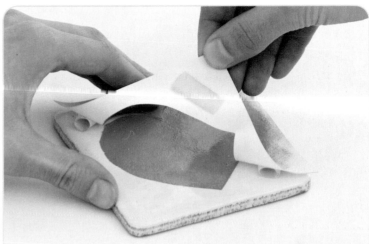

Leave to dry completely, for about 30 minutes. When the paint is dry to the touch, carefully lift the edge of the stencil and slowly peel it off, together with the masking tape.

Painting onto ceramics

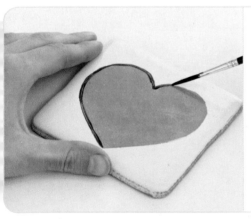

1 If you'd like to accentuate the shape, you could paint a thin line around the edge in a contrasting colour, using a fine paintbrush.

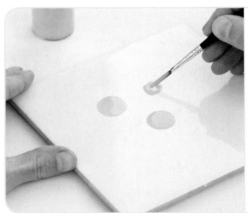

2 Achieving solid colour can be tricky with ceramic paints. Work with a loaded paintbrush and flood the area to be painted with colour.

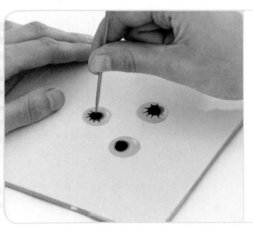

3 To achieve paint effects, you'll need to work quickly as ceramic paints become tacky soon after application. Experiment with dripping a second colour on wet paint and dragging with a cocktail stick.

FIXING CERAMIC PAINTS

Once the paints are dry, place the ceramic in a cold oven and set to the recommended temperature. Bake for the stated time, turn off the oven, and leave to cool in the oven. Do not be tempted to remove the ceramic from the oven when it is still hot as the sudden change in temperature may make it crack.

Set of coasters PROJECT

Make this fun set of four fruit-themed coasters using plain white ceramic bathroom or kitchen tiles. All four coasters require the same techniques – it's just the design that changes. Use the templates on p.90, or why not come up with your very own designs?

YOU WILL NEED

- 4 white ceramic tiles 10 x 10cm (4 x 4in)
- cloth
- white spirit
- card or thick paper
- pencil
- ruler
- scalpel and scissors
- cutting mat
- masking tape
- ceramic paints in turquoise, yellow, peridot green, and brown
- make-up sponge
- medium-size flat paintbrush
- fine paintbrush

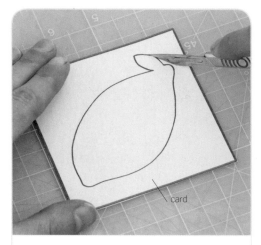

card

1 Clean the surface of the tile using a cloth dipped in white spirit. Leave to dry. Transfer the templates on p.90 onto card and cut out carefully using a scalpel, so that you have two stencils: a solid fruit shape and its frame.

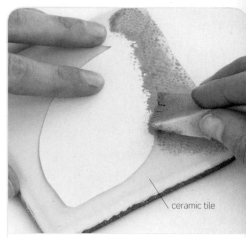

ceramic tile

2 Stick the solid fruit stencil to the tile with masking tape loops stuck on the underside of the stencil. Pressing the edges of the stencil down to avoid seepage, sponge on the turquoise paint. Leave to dry for 30 minutes, then remove the stencil.

unpainted border

3 Using a medium-size flat paintbrush, paint the body of the lemon with a generous amount of yellow paint. Leave a thin, unpainted border around the shape for effect. Rinse the brush.

4 When the yellow paint is dry, paint the leaf in peridot green using a fine paintbrush. Rinse and dry the brush, then paint the stalk brown: try to paint it in just one or two even strokes.

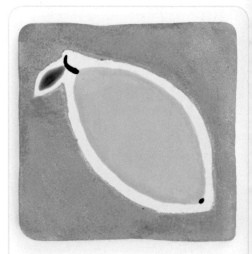

5 Leave the tile to dry for 24 hours. Repeat Steps 1 to 4 to apply the other designs to three more tiles so that you have a full set. Follow the paint manufacturer's instructions to set the colours.

Mosaics: *the direct method*

The direct method is a simple mosaic technique that is suitable for both flat and three-dimensional surfaces. One of its disadvantages, however, is that the adhesive is opaque and covers up the drawing as you work, so it's best to keep designs simple. The mosaic pieces are difficult to adjust once the adhesive has dried, so it pays to plan your piece out in advance.

Choosing your materials

Vitreous glass and unglazed ceramic are easy to cut, while marble and smalti have a traditional look and appeal. Glazed ceramic and broken china are usually coloured on one side only, so these work well with the direct method of application.

Cutting and shaping the tiles

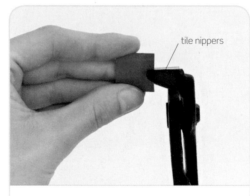

1 To achieve greater detail, quarter mosaic tiles before you begin. Place the tile nippers at the edge of the tile and squeeze gently while holding the tile with your other hand so that it does not fly away. Wear safety goggles to protect your eyes.

2 In order to create interesting patterns and representational designs, you can cut more defined shapes by placing the tile nippers at different angles and nibbling away at the edges of the tile.

Planning and transferring your design

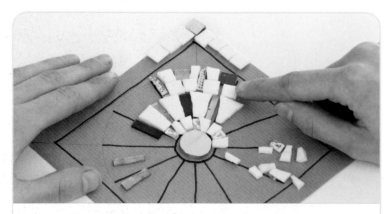

1 Draw your design on paper first. Lay out the cut tiles on your design, adjusting the colours and shapes until you are happy with the effect.

2 Copy or trace your design onto your chosen surface using a pencil or marker pen.

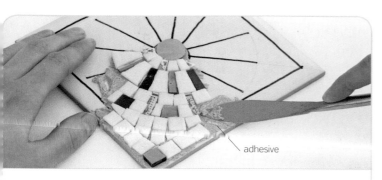

adhesive

3 Mix cement-based adhesive with water to make a thick paste. Apply to the surface of the tile, using a plasterer's small tool or palette knife. Cover a small area at a time so that the adhesive does not skin over and the design is still visible.

4 Carefully position the mosaic pieces in the adhesive bed. If you're not going to grout the tile, lay the pieces as close as possible, but if you are, leave even gaps between them. The size of gap can vary from 1 to 4mm ($\frac{1}{16}$ to $\frac{3}{16}$in) but it will look neater if the gaps are consistent.

Levelling the surface

If you're using mosaic pieces of slightly different thickness and want to achieve a flat final surface, add a little extra adhesive to the backs of the thinner pieces.

Grouting the piece

When the adhesive is dry, grout the piece. Mix the grout with water to form a thick paste and apply to the surface of the mosaic. You can use a grouting float to do this, but for small and 3D pieces it's easier to use your fingers protected by rubber gloves.

Removing excess grout

Clean off the excess grout with a damp sponge, turning the sponge over after every wipe so that you are always using a clean face. When the grout is almost dry, after about 20 minutes, clean off any surface residue with a dry cloth.

Mosaics: the indirect method

In this technique, the mosaic is made in reverse on paper before being fixed to its final position. This is a practical way of working, especially for larger projects. This method allows you to do all the cutting work while sitting comfortably at a work surface, and allows you to see the design you're following. It's also easy to make amendments as you go.

Transferring your design onto brown paper

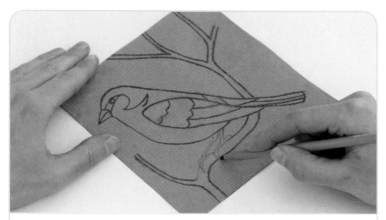

Draw the design onto brown paper, remembering to reverse it if it is not symmetrical or includes lettering. This can be done by turning over the original and tracing over it again on a lightbox or against a window.

Sticking the tiles onto the brown paper

tiles stuck face down

Apply a small amount of 50:50 washable PVA glue to water to the paper with a small brush, then apply a piece of mosaic, right side down. Repeat to complete the design. Leave to dry.

Fixing the tiles to your chosen surface

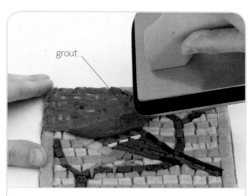

grout

1 The mosaic can now be fixed to any rigid surface such as a timber board, wall, or floor. Pre-grout the mosaic: mix the grout with water to form a thick paste and apply it to the mosaic to fill the joints. Wipe off excess grout with a damp sponge.

adhesive

2 Apply the cement-based adhesive to your chosen surface. Mix the adhesive with water to create a thick paste and comb it over the surface using a small-notched trowel to achieve a thin, even bed. Pay particular attention to the edges.

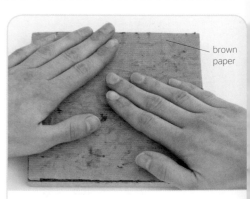

brown paper

3 Carefully pick up the mosaic and turn it over onto the adhesive. Make sure it's in place correctly, then apply gentle pressure all over to ensure that all the mosaic pieces are firmly bedded.

Removing the brown paper

1 Wet the paper with a sponge, keep the paper damp until the glue dissolves (about 15 minutes, depending on the strength of the glue and the air temperature). While waiting, apply a little more adhesive to the edges of the mosaic to strengthen them.

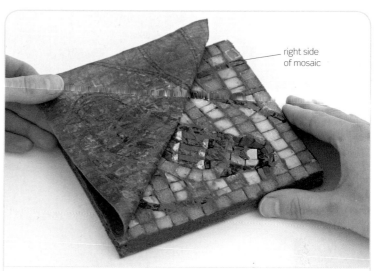

right side of mosaic

2 Lift a corner of the paper. If it comes up easily continue to peel, pulling it back parallel to the mosaic surface so as not to lift the tiles out of their bed of grout. If it's hard to peel the paper back, re-wet the surface with the sponge. Some grout will have bled through onto the surface of the tiles – wipe it off with a damp sponge before it dries. Keep turning the sponge so that you always use a clean face.

Grouting and finishing

1 Grout the front of the mosaic to fill any gaps either immediately or after the adhesive has dried. Moisten the surface of the mosaic with a damp sponge, then spread grout across the surface, working it into the gaps. Clean with a damp sponge, turning the sponge with every wipe.

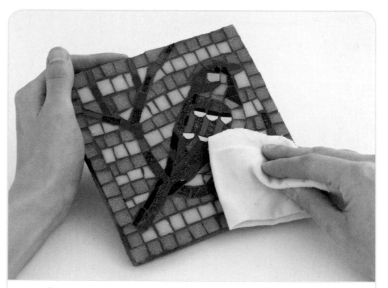

2 After about 20 minutes, when the grout has begun to dry, pass a dry cloth over the surface of the mosaic to remove any residual grout.

Mosaic bowl PROJECT

This calming, woodland-inspired mosaic bowl is made using the direct method, the simplest way of making a mosaic – this means that the tiles are glued straight onto the bowl and then grouted. It is quick and has the advantage of the work being visible as you are creating it. Put down paper or a protective cloth on your work surface before you begin making this project.

YOU WILL NEED

- pencil
- wooden bowl
- flat-backed beads and 5mm (¼in) millefiori
- green tesserae
- tile nippers
- PVA glue
- rubber gloves
- protective mask and goggles
- mosaic grout (either pre-mixed or made up following the manufacturer's instructions)
- grout spreader
- sponge
- lint-free cloth

1 Draw a wavy line onto your bowl about 4.5cm (1¾in) from the top. Draw a second line roughly 1.5cm (½in) directly below this one. Select the special tiles and embellishments that you are going to use for the accent lines and place them in groups of the same colour and type.

2 Cut some of the special tiles in half and quarters. Do this by holding the tile, square on, between thumb and forefinger, and positioning the nippers at the edge. Squeeze the nippers gently to cut the tile. Do this again to make quarter tiles. Wear goggles to protect your eyes.

3 Lay the tiles and embellishments along your wavy line in a pattern. Vary iridescent and matt tiles to create a pattern. Move the pieces off the bowl, keeping their order. Add PVA glue to the back of each piece and stick to your bowl leaving even gaps between them.

4 Starting with the lightest green tiles, cut them in half (see Step 2) and glue them on both sides of the initial accent line. Complete one line at a time, gradually increasing or decreasing the shade and adding an accent line at regular intervals until the bowl is covered. Leave to dry overnight.

5 Wearing rubber gloves and a mask, use the grout spreader to apply grout generously over the mosaic, working in different directions. Work it into all of the gaps and around the outer edge of the bowl.

6 Use a damp sponge to gently wipe away excess grout. Leave for 20 minutes, then repeat. When the grout is completely dry, use a lint-free dry cloth to wipe away any residue and polish the mosaic to a shine.

Flowerpots PROJECT

These flowerpots are embellished with a simple but effective mosaic decoration, made up of fragments of broken china and unglazed ceramic tiles. The pots used here are the plain rimless terracotta ones, but the technique works equally well on terracotta pots with rims (plastic pots are not rigid enough). The designs on the two pots echo each other: one has a blue flower design on a blue and white patterned background, while the background of the other is white and the flowers are patterned. This project uses the direct method.

YOU WILL NEED

- blue and white china plates
- towel
- hammer
- tile nippers
- 2 terracotta pots approx 15cm (6in) high
- 70:30 solution of washable PVA glue and water
- medium-size paintbrush
- pencil
- blue glass mosaic tiles
- cement-based adhesive
- plasterer's small tool or palette knife
- white grout
- sponge

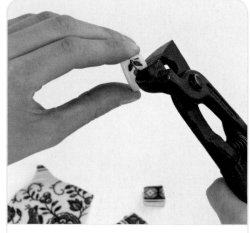

1 Wrap the china plates in a towel and smash them with a hammer. Cut the pieces into smaller, more regular shapes using tile nippers.

2 Seal the terracotta pot by painting it with the PVA solution and leave to dry.

3 Draw a simple design onto the pot in pencil and lay out the same motif on your work surface using the blue glass tiles. Cut these into strips to make the stem and into triangles for the flower and leaves.

adhesive

4 Apply cement-based adhesive to the pot's surface with a plasterer's small tool or palette knife, roughly following the design. Position the blue tile pieces on the adhesive, starting with the flower.

5 Fill in the background with pieces of broken plate. Choose pieces with a similar pattern to make a border around the rim. Apply adhesive to small areas at a time, turning the pot upside down to reach the base more easily. When the adhesive is dry, grout the piece and wipe away excess grout with a damp sponge.

Trivet PROJECT

Mosaic provides a practical wipe-clean surface and is ideal for functional pieces like this trivet. You can either use a ceramic floor tile or a wooden board base. Protect the underside with a felt backing. This project uses the indirect method.

YOU WILL NEED

- brown paper
- pencil or stick of charcoal
- approximately 270 (800g/1lb 12oz) vitreous glass tiles in orange, red, white, black, blue, and purple
- tile nippers
- 50:50 solution of washable PVA glue and water, plus extra undiluted glue
- small and medium paintbrushes
- 30 x 30cm (12 x 12in) MDF board, 12mm (½in) thick, or ceramic tile
- cement-based adhesive
- small-notched trowel
- sponge
- dark grey grout
- rubber gloves
- cloth
- 30 x 30cm (12 x 12in) piece of felt
- scissors

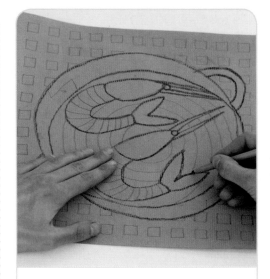

1 Transfer the template on p.91 onto brown paper using a pencil or charcoal.

2 Quarter the tiles using tile nippers. Cut thin strips for the antennae and more defined shapes for the tail. Using the small paintbrush, apply the PVA solution to a small area of the paper at a time. Start with the prawns, then work outwards to the pan, fixing the tiles right side down onto the paper.

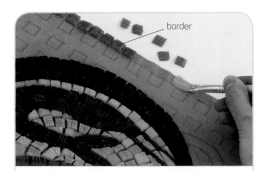

border

3 Before filling in the blue and purple checked tablecloth, lay a row of blue quartered tiles around the edge to create a neat border, then work inwards to fill in the tablecloth pattern. Once completed, leave the glue to dry. Pre-grout the mosaic.

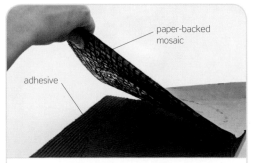

paper-backed mosaic

adhesive

4 Apply adhesive to the board or tile using the small-notched trowel. Turn the mosaic over and press onto the adhesive. Wet the paper with a damp sponge to dissolve the glue, then peel the paper off. Grout the piece and remove excess grout with a clean sponge. Wipe clean with a cloth.

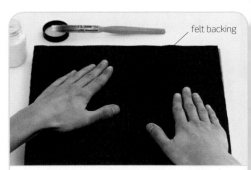

felt backing

5 Paint the underside of the board or tile with full-strength PVA and place the felt square onto it. Press down with your hands and wipe away any excess glue with a damp cloth. Allow to dry for one hour before turning over.

Templates

Coasters (pp.78–79)

Enlarge by 150% on a photocopier

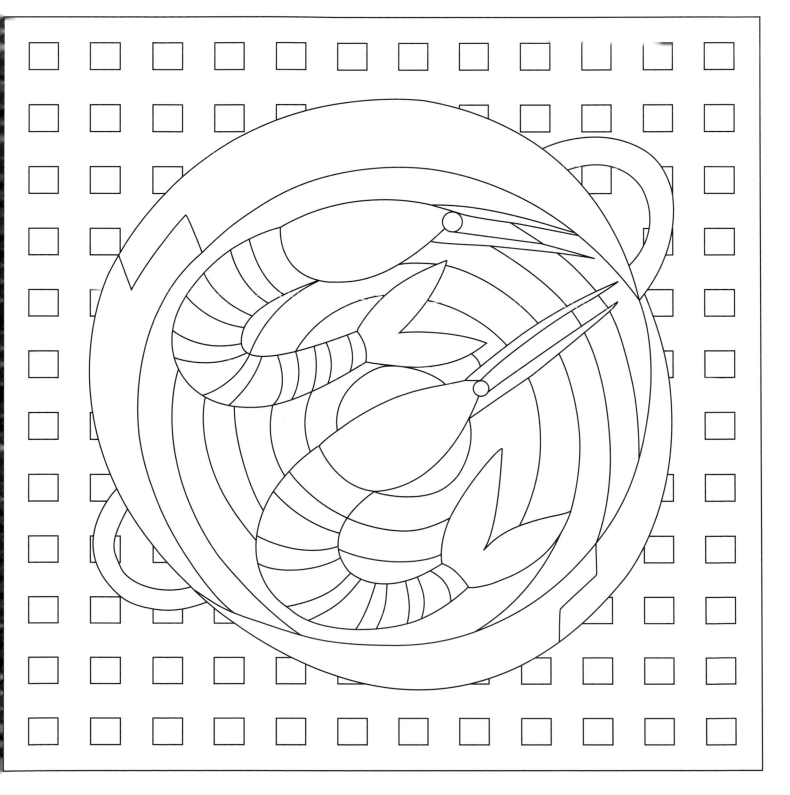

Enlarge by 150% on a photocopier

Leaf pendant (pp.60–61)

Pendant (pp.54–55)

Brooch (pp.58–59)

Tea light holder (pp.68–69)

Cuff (pp.46–47)

(Actual size not shown)

Index

The authors

A talented and dedicated team of crafters, all experts in their field, contributed towards the making of this book.

Tessa Hunkin

mosaics (direct)

mosaics (indirect)

Michael Ball

film and leadwork

Ria Holland

painting china

Helen Johannessen

painting china

painting tiles

Karen Mitchell

mosaics (direct)

Cheryl Owen

beading

silver wirework

cold enamelling

loom weaving

polymer clay

air-dry clay

metal clay

painting glass

Clara Smith

metal clay

ACKNOWLEDGMENTS

Dorling Kindersley would like to thank Fiona Corbridge for her invaluable input in the early stages of development, Ira Sharma and Era Chawla for design assistance, Jane Ewart for photography art direction, Ruth Jenkinson for photography, Carly Churchill for hand-modelling and photographic assistance, Meryl Davies for photographic assistance, Hilary Mandleberg for sense-checking, Katie Hardwicke for proofreading, Ria Holland for design assistance, and Marie Lorimer for indexing.